*The Wisdom of Carl Jung* is a brilliantly arranged selection of brief, accessible citations from the formal writings and personal letters of C. G. Jung. The short excerpts, each complete in itself, convey a direct "feel" of Jung's style and experiential way of engaging the realities of the psyche. Edward Hoffman's book is far and away the best available introduction to Jung's life-enhancing wisdom.

—Steven Joseph, M.D.
editor, *The San Francisco Jung Institute Library Journal*

D1452848

# RELATED BOOKS BY EDWARD HOFFMAN

*Ace the Corporate Personality Test*

*Future Visions: The Unpublished Papers of Abraham Maslow*

*Opening the Inner Gates: New Paths in Kabbalah and Psychology*

*Psychological Testing at Work*

*The Book of Birthday Wishes*

*The Book of Fathers' Wisdom: Paternal Advice from Moses to Bob Dylan*

*The Drive for Self: Alfred Adler and the Founding of Individual Psychology*

*The Right to Be Human: A Biography of Abraham Maslow*

*Visions of Innocence: Spiritual and Mystical Experiences of Childhood*

*The Way of Splendor: Jewish Mysticism and Modern Psychology*

*The Love Compatability Book* (with Marcella Bakur Weiner)

# The Wisdom of

# CARL JUNG

EDITED BY EDWARD HOFFMAN, PH.D.

PHILOSOPHICAL
LIBRARY

CITADEL PRESS
Kensington Publishing Corp.
www.kensingtonbooks.com

To K. Dean Stanton, friend and colleague

CITADEL PRESS BOOKS are published by

Kensington Publishing Corp.
850 Third Avenue
New York, NY 10022

First printing: March 2003

10  9  8  7  6  5  4  3  2  1

Printed in the United States of America

Library of Congress Control Number: 2002113395

ISBN 0-8065-2434-0

# CONTENTS

# PREFACE

Ever since I discovered Jung's writings when first major-
ing in psychology at Cornell University, his ideas have fascinated and inspired me. Jung's far-reaching views on
archetype, extraversion, persona, shadow, the collective unconscious, synchronicity, artistry, mythology, individuation, and mystical experience were not only intriguing, but
directly relevant to my graduate work at the University of
Michigan several years later. Especially concerning my interest in enhancing creativity via alternative education for
both children and adults, Jung's psychological system seemed
highly applicable.

And yet, I had to admit that wading into his dense, voluminous output wasn't easy. Translated from a highly academic German, Jung's many books and articles were difficult
to read. And as I completed my doctoral study and began
my professional career, I found that I wasn't alone in my reaction: many of my psychological and educational colleagues, as well as friends in other fields, viewed Jung as an
exciting thinker, but dauntingly turgid as an expositor of
his own ideas.

Whereas Freud wrote about such matters as sexuality
with poetic elegance, and Adler described family life from a
witty, avuncular perspective, Jung had no such gift for literary accessibility. Late in life, he tried to deflect such criticism by countering with the analogy that quantum physics
could hardly be "watered down," or put into simple words
for laypeople, so why should his scientific approach to the
human mind be attacked as hard to grasp?

And yet, the fact remains that it's a formidable effort for
nearly everyone to read Jung's works, however scintillating

their notions. I've long felt the need, therefore, for a lucid, compact book to present his wisdom directly—rather than through the layered viewpoints of his students and admirers. For no matter how well meaning, such volumes inevitably produce distortions. And equally important, it seems to me, has been the necessity for a contemporary anthology that could bring to bear Jung's unique insights on today's psychological and social challenges now forty years after his death at age eighty-five.

The task has been a most enjoyable one. In perusing Jung's published letters, interviews, and lectures, and of course, his collected writings, I've not only deepened my respect for the originality of Jung's system of thought, but gained an even greater awareness of its immense relevance for us today. If this book manages to share these twin perspectives, it will have fulfilled its purpose.

# ACKNOWLEDGMENTS

Though this book has been germinating in conceptual form for several years, senior editor Bob Shuman of Kensington Publishing provided the enthusiastic go-ahead, together with my literary agent Alice Martell, finally to make it happen. Editor Richard Ember ably guided the publication process.

Over the years, I've enjoyed many stimulating discussions with Dr. Gerald Epstein, Jack Fei, Marcos Florence, Dr. Steven Joseph, Dr. Ariel Maidenbaum, Dr. Ted Mann, Dr. Samuel Menahem, Paul Palnik, Dr. Russ Reeves, K. Dean Stanton, the late Alyce Tresenfeld, and Dr. Marcella Bakur Weiner on psychological topics central to this anthology. These dialogues have been a continuing source of inspiration to me. My international colleagues Professor Xu Jinsheng at the Institute for Social Science in Beijing and Professors Naoki Nomura, Shoji Muramoto, and Yoshikazu Ueda in Japan have enhanced my appreciation for cross-cultural issues in social science. As research assistants, Harvey Gitlin, Linda Joyce, and Mia Song have been eager and efficient. On the home front, I wish to thank my family for their sustained support of my therapeutic work and writing.

# Part I

## THE LIFE OF CARL JUNG

Carl Jung ranks among the greatest psychological thinkers of modern times. Alongside Sigmund Freud and his fellow Viennese physician Alfred Adler, the Swiss-born Jung is credited as one of the three founders of personality theory and psychotherapy. Yet strikingly, while Freud's system of psychoanalysis has fallen into disrepute, and Adler's approach called individual psychology has been absorbed into child guidance and family counseling, and his own work largely forgotten, Jung has become more influential than ever since his death in 1961. Not only in North America and Europe, but increasingly around the globe, Jung's ideas about our inner world are now exerting unprecedented impact.

For example, the Myers-Briggs Type Indicator that derives from Jungian theory is the most widely used personality instrument in the world. Likewise, Jung's fascinating notions about inner growth and wholeness, aging, and mystical experiences like synchronicity, have affected not only professional fields encompassing counseling, education, psychology, psychotherapy, and theology, but also our wider culture today.

Whereas Freud and his followers largely feared anything that deviated from Western rationalism, Jung viewed spirituality and imagination as vital, creative forces. His lifetime of exploration into such ancient systems of knowledge as Taoism and the *I Ching,* Yoga and Hindu meditation, and Kabbalah and Gnosticism, has immensely broadened the science of the human psyche.

Like other great visionaries, Carl Jung was often misunderstood and maligned for much of his long career. His pursuits into mythology, alchemy, and comparative religion frequently made his name taboo in more conservative psychology circles. He was typically dismissed as a "mystic" for espousing unorthodox and radical ideas about the human mind. Yet Jung never ceased to point out that science has nearly always labeled as "mystical" or "superstitious" what it initially could not comprehend. Toward the end of his life, he repeatedly warned that our willful failure to acknowledge, much less confront, our dark, shadowy side, had produced two world wars and might well result in a nuclear Armaggedon. Nevertheless, he was hopeful that the importance of his discoveries concerning our vast unconscious within might be recognized and heeded before another calamity.

Originally groomed by Freud himself to be the heir to the psychoanalytic throne, Jung soon spurned the Freudian crown and its narrow kingdom. For the young Swiss psychiatrist had glimpsed the much wider and more dazzling lands that lay outside the bounds of psychoanalysis. After his soul-wrenching break with Freud, Jung journeyed far inward and thereupon marked his own path—rather separate from both conventional psychotherapy and academia—for the rest of his life. In dozens of publications, spanning sixty years, he developed a complex and multitiered approach to our inner world. He often regarded his life as a myth; in his last few years, he seemed to have indeed personified the mythological character of the timeless Wise Old Man.

In the forty years since Jung's death at age eighty-six, his stature has steadily grown. His own writings remain a formidable body (the *Collected Works* consist of twenty-one detailed volumes) and one certainly not easy to grasp in its entirety. But his ideas are increasingly influencing mainstream psychology and the larger culture, through the writing and teaching of his many articulate students and colleagues.

From Carl Jung's initial findings on mental complexes and behavior to his later, daring speculations on our transcendent relation to time, space, and causality—his insights are still vital and alive. They cut across a variety of seemingly disparate fields of knowledge. In a time of perhaps unprecedented spiritual upheaval around the globe, Jung's patient excavations of our hidden capabilities—and their age-old connections—may prove to be his greatest legacy.

## ANCESTRY AND YOUTH

Carl Gustav Jung came from a highly educated and intellectual family of Swiss-German background. His paternal grandfather, whose name the great thinker bore, was a famous medical professor at the University of Basel in Switzerland. The son of a well-known physician (though also rumored to be an illegitmate child of Goethe), Carl Jung Sr. (1795–1864) was a poet and a political freethinker too. He was beloved as a benefactor to the town where he taught for many decades. Among his projects there, he founded a hospital for emotionally disturbed children. Over the course of three marriages (he was twice widowed), he sired thirteen children. The youngest of these was Paul Jung, Carl's father.

The other grandfather, Samuel Preiswerk, was a high-ranking minister in the Swiss church, as well as a gifted Hebrew scholar and a poet. Interestingly, he believed strongly in spiritualist phenomena and the reality of unseen forces. However, both men died before Carl was born and their influence on him was therefore only indirect.

Paul Jung (1842–1896) led a rather undistinguished life. Trained as a parson, he married Emilie Preiswerk and served as the vicar of Kesswil, the Swiss village where Carl was born in 1875. In Paul's youth, he had shown promise in Oriental languages and completed a thesis on the Arabic version of the Song of Songs. But according to Carl, his father never developed his mental faculties and remained a provincial country parson until his death. In retrospect, his son viewed him as a weak, almost pathetic figure—plagued by both an unhappy marriage and constant religious doubts. "His days of glory had ended with his final [school] examinations," Carl Jung curtly remarked decades later. "Thereafter, he forgot his linguistic talent."[1]

In his autobiographical account, *Memories, Dreams, and Reflections*, Jung went on to describe his mother as a perplexing mixture of superficiality and depth. On the surface, she appeared "a kindly . . . fat woman, extremely hospitable, and [the] possessor of a great sense of humor."[2] Beneath that exterior, though, he occasionally felt the presence of a highly astute, knowing individual. He was always reticent to recall his parents' persistent marital conflicts; consequently, we know little about their relationship other than they frequently quarreled and had at least one major separation.

Carl's boyhood was a rather solitary one. He was an only child for nine years until his sister Johanna Gertrud was born. A much simpler, less intellectual person than Carl, she greatly admired her distinguished brother and lived in his shadow all her life. From Carl's own reminscences and from those who knew him as a child, he was somewhat introverted, given to a good deal of introspection about spiritual questions. In view of the intensely sectarian atmosphere of his family—no less than eight uncles were parsons, besides his father—this fact is hardly surprising. He inwardly rebelled against much of the authoritarian dogma the adults around him espoused.

At the age of eleven, Carl's vistas were suddenly widened when he entered the Gymnasium in Basel. There, the poor, local preacher's son encountered well-dressed boys who exuded the casual air of wealth and sophistication. With his worn trousers and shoes with holes in them, he inevitably became the butt of many jokes. However, his sheer physical size discouraged very much active bullying.

Nevertheless, for nearly a year, Carl suffered from fainting spells and other nervous ailments that kept him out of school. From his later recollections, it seems clear that the illness was mainly psychosomatic and perhaps even a form of school phobia.

Scholastically, as a youth Carl Jung was gifted in writing and an omnivorous reader. Overall, though, he was only a fair to poor student, with special difficulties in mathematics and grammar. Several of his teachers during his adolescence frankly regarded the parson's son as mentally deficient, though slowly his studies improved with age.

Not unexpectedly, Carl's parents worried over his career goals as his graduation eventually neared. They could not hope to support him for many more years. Carl felt drawn to the adventures of empirical science as well as to the mysteries of comparative religion. Initially, he planned to be an archaeologist and read widely in philosophy and classical thought. He was relieved that his father advised him, "Be anything you like except a theologian."[3] After much reflection, Carl decided on medicine for its practical advantages. In the spring of 1895, following his matriculation from the Gymnasium, he registered as a student at the University of Basel Medical School. He was then nineteen and was twenty after his first semester, about the usual age for studies at the time.

Carl Jung's five years in medical school were a maturing period for him. Much of his adolescent shyness vanished as a new, confident personality began to emerge. He must have felt a special pride, too, in studying at the university where his grandfather had so distinguished himself as a faculty member. But in 1896, Carl's father died from cancer. The family was now faced with economic hardship and it seemed doubtful whether Carl could even continue his expensive medical schooling. With the help of relatives, he and his family managed to scrape by financially. While living at home, Carl also worked for an aunt selling antiques and proved himself an excellent young businessman. He was now quite a physically imposing figure, over six feet one inches tall, with a deep resonant voice and a commanding manner.

As a university student, Carl blossomed intellectually. Besides his regular studies, he often presented talks on science, psychology, and religion before student groups and was elected president of the student association—following a heated campaign. At this germinating stage in his career, Carl Jung was already controversial in his beliefs and antagonized some of his peers with his fiery polemics against the materialist outlook in science. During these years, his interest bloomed in what William James called the "romantic" or "night" side of the human psyche—encompassing such intriguing realms as trance and mediumistic states, hypnosis and hallucinations, and parapsychology. He avidly consumed many works on spiritualist and mystical phenomena. Even at this age, he was convinced that we possess inner capacities rarely used in everyday life.

While in medical training, Carl experienced several unusual events that further aroused his interest in the paranormal. At home one day, as he sat studying, a sturdy walnut table resounded like a pistol shot and split down the middle. No one was nearby. Two weeks later, Carl returned from class to find the entire household in an uproar. Without any warning, another deafening report had resounded through the house, this time from the direction of a heavy kitchen sideboard. Within it, Carl found that the steel blade of a bread knife had shattered into three distinct pieces. Taking the broken knife to a cutler the next day, Carl learned to his amazement that the blade was technically sound and could only have been broken deliberately and with effort. No one in the house seemed to have caused the damage. Carl considered this incident incredible and deeply symbolic of how little we really know about the universe. He carefully kept the pieces of the knife for the rest of his life.

Soon after these strange happenings, Carl decided to attend a series of séances given by a teenage girl related to him. For two years, he regularly observed these "sittings"—not unlike those William James was witnessing a continent away in Boston—and maintained a detailed diary of each séance. While he found that most of his cousin's "visions" and discourses could be traced back to experiences in her life and even to outright trickery, he felt sure there was a genuine element of paranormal knowledge in her trances. Approximately three years later, the case would form the basis for Carl's doctoral thesis and first publication. It was entitled *On the Psychology and Pathology of So-Called Occult Phenomena*.

By this time, graduation from medical school was approaching and Carl had still not chosen a field of specialization. His closest professors encouraged him to specialize in internal medicine and secured for him an assistantship in Munich. However, just before his final, comprehensive examinations, he skimmed a psychiatry textbook by Krafft-Ebing and like a thunderbolt suddenly knew that his future lay in this fledgling discipline. Carl easily passed his examinations. But to the shock and anger of faculty and friends, he decided to pursue a career in psychiatry—perhaps the least prestigious field of medicine at the time.

## BURGHOLZI PSYCHIATRIC HOSPITAL: FIRST DISCOVERIES

In December 1900, Carl Jung arrived at Burgholzi Psychiatric Hospital, not far from the city of Zurich. Despite his frequent travels abroad in years to come, this scenic locale would always remain the Swiss visionary's home. A tall, energetic young man of twenty-five, Jung was eager to begin his first professional position. He was an assistant to Eugen Bleuer, the influential but dour medical director of Burgholzi.

The facility itself was among the most modern and progressive of psychiatric hospitals in the world. The staff boasted an international reputation. Yet psychiatric knowledge was almost nonexistent at the turn of the century, and treatment was equally barren. "From the clinical point of view which then prevailed, the human personality of the patient, his individuality, did not matter,"[4] Jung recalled decades later. In a monastic-like atmosphere, the resident physicians lived on grounds with their patients, were scrupulously forbidden alcohol, and were expected to be back promptly in their quarters when the main gates of the hospital closed each evening at ten o'clock.

From the beginning of his work with the severely mentally ill, Jung was struck by how little his colleagues knew about the human mind. He read virtually every book in the field he could lay his hands on, including the somewhat disreputable writings of Sigmund Freud, whom most physicians still regarded as a crank. In the winter of 1902–1903, Jung made a further effort to increase his knowledge by spending several months in Paris to study with Pierre Janet, a leading psychiatric researcher. Not long after Jung's return, he set up a laboratory at Burgholzi for experimenting on the nature of mental illness. That same year of 1905, he was promoted to senior psychiatrist at the University of Zurich.

Among Jung's first professional innovations was the use of the word association test as a means to tap one's unconscious thoughts and feelings. With this procedure, a series of stimulus words are read aloud, one at a time. The person is asked to respond with the first word that comes to mind; each response is timed. This test had already been in existence for some decades, but it had been utilized to examine only conscious lines of thought. Jung's innovation had been to employ the test to investigate abnormalities in reaction, thereby making the test available as a tool to explore the roots of emotional disturbance.

Thus, through the individual's specific verbal associations and response time, previously hidden emotional conflicts or fantasies could now be uncovered and probed. For example, aggressive responses and long reaction times to the words "mother," "wife," and "breast" might signify that the patient had unconscious hostilities toward women. Jung thereupon developed the term *complex* to describe this sort of hidden, emotionally charged set of associations.

Jung found the test particularly useful in making more accessible the inner states of his schizophrenic patients, who were typically withdrawn and reclusive. In the relatively brief time it took to administer the test, he could learn at least partially what might be disturbing them. Based on this research, he next came to the insight that within the madness of his patients' bizarre statements, there lay a kernel of quite comprehensible feeling—but that decoding was necessary to interpret these verbalizations.

For instance, a woman might repeatedly scream that she was "condemned like Socrates." Actually, Jung argued, she was declaring that she felt condemned by her family just as Socrates had been judged and sentenced to die by the government. Therefore, the young psychiatrist urged that his colleagues carefully attend to the meaning—indeed often veiled—of what each patient was saying. Of course, this notion has become a therapeutic mainstay. In 1907, his first major work, focusing on these early concerns, was published. It was entitled *The Psychology of Dementia Praecox* (a term now replaced by *schizophrenia*).

During these years, Carl Jung was also quite active romantically. Following his trip to Paris in 1903, he married Emma Rauschenbach, daughter of a wealthy Swiss-German industrial family. Initially, Emma had turned down Carl's marriage proposal but relented after his sustained wooing. Three children were born to them over the next five years (two more would later arrive), but it was not until 1909 that they left their cramped apartment at the Burgholzi Psychiatric Hospital and moved into their own, newly built house on Lake Zurich. By then, Carl had begun to attain international recognition and was able to open a full-time private practice besides his teaching duties. He had also become a key figure in Freud's growing psychoanalytic movement. Photographs of the young couple during this period reveal an attractive though hardly beautiful woman several years younger than her tall, sturdy husband.

## JUNG AND FREUD

The subject of Jung's relationship with Freud is one still embroiled in controversy. Although more than ninety-five years have elapsed since these two intellectual giants first crossed paths, their passionate friendship and subsequent break continues to generate a steady stream of scholarly analysis. Supporters in each of their schools still trade insults, rumors, and accusations about their involvements. In Jung's own life, he arrived at a mature, reflective reminiscence of Freud's greatness and limitations. However, for many decades Jung carried with him an obvious bitterness over the failed relationship.

As early as 1900, Carl Jung was aware of Freud's work through his first major book, *The Interpretation of Dreams*, published that year. Apparently, though, the volume made little impression on Jung at the time. Several years later, he suddenly discovered in Freud's case narratives a striking similarity to findings obtained through the word association test and other investigative tools—above all, that we each have an unconscious mind that suppresses emotional matters from our conscious awareness.

In early 1906, Jung hesitantly sent his *Diagnostic Association Studies* to Freud—who was definitely *persona non grata* in the academic world. The young Swiss psychiatrist (nearly twenty years Freud's junior) was painfully aware that his involvement with this unorthodox Viennese physician might prove professionally damaging, but nevertheless initiated the correspondence. Freud reciprocated immediately by mailing a packet of his articles. He was eager if not desperate for greater recognition and particularly for allies. Thus, with the articles he penned a note declaring that, "I am confident that you will often be in a position to back me up."[5] Jung's intuitions soon proved correct. Before long, his spirited defense of Freud's work began to create him enemies and in fact block his own academic advancement.

From the beginning, their relationship was a powerful mixture of both intellectual and emotional attraction. Within a few months, their correspondence took on a lively and even intimate character. They viewed themselves as pioneers in the exploration of the human mind. In early 1907, they first met at Freud's home in Vienna and spent thirteen hours engrossed in conversation. Undoubtedly, there was a heady father-son magnetism in the friendship. Soon, Freud was referring to his Swiss colleague as his "scientific heir"; Jung had probably long been searching for the spiritual mentor his father had failed to be. Decades later, he recalled:

> Freud was the first man of real importance I had encountered in my experience up to that time; no one else could compare with him . . . I found him extremely intelligent, shrewd and altogether remarkable.[6]

Over the years, their letters to each other reflected their growing mutual enchantment. In the spring of 1908, Jung organized the First International Congress of Psychoanalysis in Salzburg. He even insisted on naming it "The Conference for Freudian Psychology." In turn, Freud disregarded the protests of his loyal Viennese contingent and appointed Jung as editor of the group's new journal. Freud now regarded the correspondence as vital to his own work and even sent telegrams when his younger colleague was tardy in responding.

In March 1909, they again met at Freud's home. By this time, the differences between them that would eventually prove insurmountable were just starting to become apparent to both men. During this meeting they argued over the importance of the sexual drive—and also the reality of paranormal phenomena. To Jung's dismay, Freud maintained a skeptical and materialist outlook. Then, suddenly, noises resounded from Freud's bookcase—suggesting "poltergeists" to Jung and proof of what he was saying. The same evening, Freud vowed to make his protégé "successor and crown prince"[7] to the psychoanalytic throne.

That summer, Professor Calvin Hall of Clark University independently invited the two researchers to speak at the school's twentieth anniversary in Worcester, Massachusetts. Jung and Freud traveled together for the journey and analyzed each other's dreams along the way. The trip was a momentous one for Jung. He met with William James and spent hours discussing philosophy, mysticism, and parapsychology. It is fascinating to speculate what these two geniuses might have accomplished together had James not died less than a year later. Both men shared an exciting vision of our inner potential—a vista far exceeding Freud's narrow view that sexuality and its repression determine our complete nature. Interestingly, James's old friend Théodore Flournoy would soon ignite Jung's lifetime interest in that side of our psyche which is expressed in dreams, visions, trances, and mythology.

Upon returning to Europe, Jung was now set to embark on intense study of symbolism and spirituality. "I had the feeling that I had caught a glimpse of a new, unknown country," he wrote, "from which swarms of new ideas flew to meet me."[8] He realized that Freud had limitations as a man—and more important—as a thinker. Yet the break between the two men took place gradually, over the next four years.

In the spring of 1910, Freud crowned Jung the first president of the International Psychoanalytic Association. "My dear Jung," he recalled Freud as urging, "promise me never to abandon the sexual theory. That is the most essential thing of all. You see, we must make a dogma out of it, an unshakable bulwark." When the astonished Swiss thinker asked him, "A bulwark—against what?" The reply was, "Against the black tide of mud—of occultism."[9] Apparently, he was referring to Jung's growing interest in mysticism and mythology. Over the strenuous objections of his Viennese disciples, Freud feverishly insisted that Jung, as a Gentile, was their best hope to spread the psychoanalytic gospel to the non-Jewish world.

During the next several years, Jung boldly pushed on with his explorations into ancient Eastern religion, Gnosticism, and Western esoteric thought. His studies intensified. Then he read Théodore Flournoy's fascinating case report of a schizophrenic woman's fantasies. They exhibited a striking similarity to the mythological motifs Jung had analyzed in religion—and convinced him that we have a natural ability to create myths out of our inner experience. He argued that such myths may be beneficial to us, invigorating our mundane lives with a sense of meaning and purpose. Humanity's quest for the divine, he stressed, had brought many valuable insights to the world and to the field of modern psychology as well. It was high time for the young science to recognize this fact.

In 1911, the Swiss iconoclast published the first part of his new book, later translated into English as *Symbols of Transformation*. In 1912, the second, more important section was issued. It hit the Freudian camp like a bombshell. Jung disputed his mentor's most cherished notions and even suggested that our sexual desires may ultimately reflect spiritual, transcendent yearnings. In a series of lectures at

Fordham University, Jung also denied the universality of the Oedipal complex—another key element of psychoanalysis.

Freud was outraged. His favorite "son" had clearly gone past the point of no return. Freud personally ridiculed Jung's book, as did his followers; they dismissed it as superstitious nonsense. In a letter to a colleague, Freud lashed out, "As regards Jung, he seems all out of his wits, he is behaving quite crazy . . . Take no more steps to his conciliation, it is to no effect."[10] The two men last met in the fall of 1913; their weak attempt at reconciliation was inevitably a failure. As though sensing exactly what Freud wished, Jung resigned from his editorship of the psychoanalytic journal and a few months later abandoned the presidency of the International Association.

## INNER JOURNEYS

Jung's excommunication from the Freudian fold left him badly shaken for several years. Torn out of a professional context that had nurtured him since his early thirties, he found himself alone in Zurich with no one remotely connected to Freud. Many of Jung's patients as well as colleagues deserted him. Yet out of his confusion and at times despair, he was propelled into his most creative and exciting work. Decades later, he was able to gaze back to this phase of his life and observe:

> The years when I was pursuing my inner images were the most important in my life—in them everything essential was decided.
>
> It all began then; the later details are only supplements and clarifications of the material that burst forth from the unconscious, and at times swamped me. It was the *prima materia* for a lifetime's work."[11]

In a way, Jung was experiencing what people today often call a "midlife crisis." Thirty-eight years old, he was outwardly the picture of success: an affluent physician with a wife and a brood of children, even a large beautiful house on a lake. Inwardly, though, none of that was what it seemed. He was unsure of his professional direction, had embarked on at least one extramarital affair (with a patient, Toni Wolfe, who became a life-long collaborator), and often felt the noisy company of his children as unbearable.

Because Jung had the courage to face this contradiction—and confront his inner voices—he succeeded in mastering them. In his own view, without this painful self-analysis, which lasted from three to six years, he could never have hit upon and developed his greatest discoveries. Today, when so many people now leap to drugs or alcohol at the slightest twinge of self-doubt, Jung's steady journey within—what he called his "confrontation with the unconscious"—offers a dramatic lesson.

Among Carl Jung's initial efforts at self-understanding was to pay special attention to his dreams. Vivid, enigmatic, at times frightening, they chiefly revealed to him the extent of his inner disorientation. In the fall of 1913, he also had the first of a series of dreams and "visions" in which he saw Europe engulfed in a tidal wave of bloody corpses. At the time, he interpreted these images as references to his own terribly depressed state—which he felt as bordering on insanity. Years later, he would also view these dreams as partly prophetic, for World War I suddenly erupted nine months later.

Simultaneously, Jung began to systematically review his entire life, from his early childhood to his present age. As thoroughly as possible, he tried to find the causes of his deep emotional turmoil. Twice, he underwent this laborious process but emerged disappointed each time, having gained no further insight. He could only conclude to himself, "Since I know nothing at all, I shall simply do whatever occurs to me. Thus, I consciously submit . . . myself to the impulses of the unconscious."[12]

Thereupon, Jung resigned from his teaching position at the University of Zurich and embraced his childhood love of building make-believe castles and towers. Despite his embarrassment at the play—after all, he was a mature physician, not a boy—he spent hours each week constructing by the lake a toy village made out of stones. Jung found the project strangely calming—so much so, in fact, that he later used sculpting as a form of therapy with patients. At the time, the notion that we as adults might mentally grow from such play was quite radical. Yet Jung trusted his own intuition.

During this period, the Swiss iconoclast also began to keep a diary or journal of his inner expeditions. Unsure whether permanent madness would be his fate—like that of several colleagues—he felt that a written record would be a signpost to others as to what he had witnessed on his perilous path within. He set down his fantasies in a diary he called his Black Book and elaborated on them with paintings and drawings. In another diary, the Red Book, Jung recorded similar fantasies in medieval script. Here, too, he instinctively devised a powerful, new tool for self-knowledge and creativity. Of course, many persons had kept a journal before Jung, but he was the first modern psychologist to seize the method as a therapeutic instrument. Later, in the 1960s and 1970s, his student, Dr. Ira Progoff, substantially expanded its use through his own cogent writings and workshops.

At times, Jung's "confrontation with his unconscious" produced strange streams of words and sentences resembling automatic writing. The language was in a stilted form, which he personally found distasteful. Toward the end of his painful inner travels, he spontaneously set down a remarkable prose poem entitled *Septem Sermones ad Mortuous* ("Seven Sermons to the Dead"). As though recording the eerie Kabbalistic message of long-departed spirits, the poem proclaimed, "We have come back from Jerusalem where we found not what we sought."[13] In years to come, Jung would devote serious attention to Gnosticism and Jewish mysticism.

By opening the doors to his unconscious, Carl Jung found himself at times surrounded by fantasy figures. In some respects, he was indeed quite close to insanity as he "heard" or "saw" legendary characters beckoning to communicate with him. Initially, two specific figures—a young woman and an old man—appeared to him. They identified themselves as Salome and Elijah. Eventually, this latter character was transformed into Philemon, the wise old man whom Faust murdered in Goethe's work. Philemon was apparently as real to Jung as imaginary playmates are to some young children and would instruct the Swiss psychiatrist about the mysterious realms beyond our conscious ego. Many of Philemon's lessons were so unusual and compelling to Jung that he soon became convinced that they originated in a source which transcended his own personality. If strangers had visited his house, they would have been startled to see the eminent physician walking about in his garden, carrying on lively, earnest conversations with this fictitious spiritual tutor.

It was while embarked on this extraordinary inner voyage that Jung created one of his most far-reaching and important techniques: namely, that of *active imagination*. For with his strong sense of identity, he was not content to passively let these fantasy figures float by him. Rather, he decided to actively engage them—as the Biblical Jacob is said to have wrestled all night with his angel.

For example, Jung experienced one fantasy in which he was exploring a remote valley inhabited by a primitive people. He came upon some hieroglyphics carved in stone but could not decipher the writing. As the letters were rather illegible too, he began to deepen them carefully with a chisel and hammer. When a nearby medicine man suddenly cried out that a splinter had pierced his eye, Jung seized him and refused to remove the shard until the shaman deciphered the script. When he reluctantly did so—and Jung thereupon understood the message from his unconscious—the whole scene abruptly vanished. Years later, the brilliant innovator explained:

> A fantasy is more or less your own invention and remains on the surface of personal things and conscious expectations. But Active Imagination, as the term denotes, means that the images have a life of their own and that the symbolic events develop according to their own logic. . . . You begin by concentrating on a mental picture (and) it begins to stir, the image becomes enriched by details, it moves and develops.[14]

Today, this powerful therapeutic tool is gaining an increasing role across many fields of psychology and medicine. Known in related guises as "guided imagery," "creative visualization," or "waking dream therapy," this method of actively engaging and elaborating our fantasies has been proven an effective treatment for heart disease, high blood pressure, and even other illnesses such as cancer. The key premise of this approach parallels Jung's bold insight that we need not fear our unconscious, for fantasy and imagination have many beneficial powers.

Yet another of Carl Jung's innovations from this time was his discovery that art has tremendous healing potential. From his early days of this period, he found that when he drew his fantasies and images within, he gave them a form of objectivity outside his psyche, thereby reducing some of his anxiety. While commander of a British internment camp in Switzerland in 1917–1918, he found himself moved each morning to sketch a new circular drawing in his notebook. The picture he repeatedly drew was a *mandala* (Sanskrit for "circle"), and it seemed to correspond somehow to his inner state. It also radiated a strong, calming influence. For the rest of his life, Jung would view the *mandala* as a spontaneous symbol—present in all cultures and historical periods—of our potentialities for wholeness and peace. This capacity he called the Self.

As a founder of art therapy, Jung encouraged his patients to draw such figures. He also emphasized that their appearance in our dreams and fantasies heralds new creativity and direction. Indeed, by the end of World War I, Jung had clearly mastered his inner voices and emerged victorious from his "confrontation with the unconscious." He now possessed a clear, unshakable vision of the human psyche and its awesome expanse.

### RISING FAME

Despite the emphasis that Carl Jung placed on his internal struggles during these years, he was hardly an idle recluse. As he traveled more deeply inward, his skill as a therapist steadily grew. So did his private practice. Through his efforts at self-healing, he felt increasingly constrained by the limitations of the Freudian approach to psychotherapy. Perhaps he was also eager to shed all party ties to the psychoanalytic movement that had rejected him. In any event, the Swiss psychiatrist introduced several revisions into the structure of modern psychotherapy.

Jung dispensed with the couch favored by his mentor and instead sat on a chair so that he could directly face the patient. He sometimes even treated patients on board his boat as they sailed around serene Lake Zurich. Jung stressed his patients' current problems far more than their childhood memories. And quite significantly, he argued that therapist and patient might profitably relate to one another outside of the consulting office. At the time, therapeutic innovators like Alfred Adler espoused a similar view. Today, however, such involvement is therapeutically and ethically banned because of the problems that arise when therapists and patients weaken professional boundaries between themselves.

Thus, in 1916, Carl Jung founded a Psychological Club in Zurich for those interested in his budding psychology. He was greatly assisted in this enterprise by Edith McCormick, daughter of John D. Rockefeller and a former patient of Jung's. She generously endowed the fledgling organization with a considerable fortune—to cover both its ongoing expenses and the purchase of a house to be used for lectures, parties, and special readings. The original building is still utilized by the Psychological Club and the C. G. Jung Institute (formed several decades later). Between 1917 and 1920, Jung's growing fame as a therapist drew many new and distinguished patients—including James Joyce's daughter and Sir Montagu Norman, the governor of the Bank of London. Jung had clearly surmounted his ostracism from the Freudian circle.

In the years corresponding to his painful midlife crisis, Carl Jung also published a variety of articles and presented occasional lectures before interested colleagues. Gradually, he came to realize that he was developing an entirely new approach to the human mind—an orientation with a spiritual outlook far more comprehensive than Freud's. The Swiss thinker coined many terms to explain his bold ideas; but in essence, they all rested on his conviction—alien to psychoanalysis—that below our personal unconscious lies an incredibly, almost unfathomably, deep realm that all humanity shares.

This region he called the *collective unconscious* and likened it to the instinctual realm that influences the behavior of lower animals. In a vivid description, which resembles William James's view, Jung later stated:

> The deepest we can reach in our exploration of the unconscious is the layer where man is no longer a distinct individ-

ual, but where his mind widens out and merges into the mind of mankind . . . where we are all the same. As the body has its anatomical conformity in its two eyes and ears and one heart and so on with only slight individual differences, so has the mind its basic conformity.[15]

Within this vast treasurehouse exist specific patterns that lead us to perceive and act in certain timeless ways—patterns he called *archetypes*.

For instance, the character of Philemon represented the sagelike part of our psyche and usually appears to us as a Wise Old Man. Salome signified the feminine side or *anima* in each male, while women perceive a masculine figure in their dreams or fantasies, reflecting their *animus* or "male" component. Similarly, our violent, animalistic impulses loom in dreams and myths as the Shadow; our noble, striving feelings appear in the form of a youthful Hero, and so on.

Based on his wide reading of mythology and comparative religion, Jung insisted that since time immemorial the task for each of us has been to blend these diverse parts of our nature into one powerful, united Self. This process, which he regarded as a lifetime one, he called *individuation*. And, he taught, the world's great religions have intuitively always known this truth and expressed it through myths and visions. Hence, he urged that we explore the spiritual traditions of the past to better understand our own inner nature. "On this collective level," he observed, "we are no longer separate individuals, we are one."[16]

In 1921, Jung published his most important work to date. *Psychological Types* was an impressive piece of scholarship, encompassing over seven hundred pages and scores of references to philosophers and theologians, Eastern and Western, spanning the centuries. A major portion of the book derived from William James's notions on the "tough-minded" versus the "tender-minded" approach to knowledge. For it was Jung's contention that our makeup within greatly influences the way we look at both facts and values. "The work sprang originally from my need to define the ways in which my outlook differed from Freud's or Adler's,"[17] he wrote. "It is one's psychological type which from the outset determines and limits a person's judgment."[18]

In this erudite volume, the Swiss psychiatrist identified the *introvert* and *extravert* as two fundamentally different styles of relating to the world around us. He saw the *introvert* as one who relies primarily on inner reality for direction; the *extravert* inherently distrusts it and instead relies on physical certainties. Jung later demarked four additional mental styles within each of these two broad categories— *thinking, sensation, feeling,* and *intuition*—so that eight "psychological types" in all were described.

Because of its handy labeling format, the book quickly won Jung an increasing following. His theory seemed to explain why people of equally high intelligence might experience tremendous difficulty in becoming friends or even in working together amicably. Of course, humanity cannot so easily be categorized into eight types of individuals; for this reason, *Psychological Types* was rightfully criticized from the outset. Yet Jung's intention was to organize in some way a vast amount of clinical observation. "For instance," he argued in later defending his system, "if you have to explain a wife to a husband or a husband to a wife, it is often very helpful to have these objective criteria, otherwise the whole thing remains 'He said'—'She said.' "[19]

## THE SEEKER ABROAD

During the 1920s and 1930s, Carl Jung went on several expeditions to civilizations outside of our Western urban world. In particular, his investigations into ancient Eastern religions prompted him to actively experience alien ways of viewing the cosmos. He also hoped to find new evidence for his belief in the existence of timeless archetypes below the surface of our everyday conscious mind. Jung's travels, while relatively brief, left him a lifetime's legacy and intensified his studies. Consequently, they greatly shaped the course of modern humanistic psychology.

Jung's first exotic trip was to North Africa in 1920. Accompanied by several friends, he traveled through Algeria and Tunisia. "This Africa is incredible," he excitedly wrote his wife back in Zurich. "Unfortunately, I cannot write coherently to you for it is all too much."[20] A few days later, he added, "I do not know what Africa is really saying to me, but it speaks."[21]

Because Jung spoke no Arabic, he was little able to communicate with the people he encountered. Instead, he had to be content to observe their nonverbal gestures and facial expressions. Imposing as a giant to the smaller Arabs, he sat quietly for hours at their coffee houses and soon realized, "What the Europeans regard as Oriental calm and apathy seemed to me a mask; behind I sensed a restlessness, a degree of agitation which I could not explain."[22]

One of the Swiss thinker's main insights there was the awareness of how vigorously our days are ruled by the clock. Son of a people famous for their watches, he suddenly saw his ever-present timepiece through the eyes of a wholly different culture. He began to ponder for the first time the nature of subjective or "interior" time. Interestingly, he also experienced the strange phenomenon that time does not always flow at an even rhythm. "The deeper we penetrated into the Sahara," he reminisced, "the more time slowed down for me; it even threatened to move backward."[23] Occasionally, he felt transported to another epoch of human history—one with an emotional intensity absent in our technological society.

The mystery of time continued to fascinate Jung. The

summer after his trip to Africa, he seized on the Chinese *I Ching* (Book of Changes), sensing that this ancient volume of divination was based on a radically non-Western conception of time. Day after day, Jung experimented with the *I Ching*. Soon, he was certain that it offered a tremendous source of wisdom to Westerners as well as Orientals. He discovered that its key premise is that our lives—mirroring the universe—are filled with countless cycles. The better able we are to discern these patterns, the greater our sense of direction and happiness.

In 1923, while still delving into Chinese philosophy, Jung met Richard Wilhelm, a renowned sinologist of German extraction. Originally a Christian missionary to China, Wilhelm translated the *I Ching* into German in the 1920s, greatly arousing Jung's interest in Eastern mysticism. The two men became very close friends and shared many exciting discussions on the relevance of the ancient Oriental disciplines for the West today. Jung and Wilhelm must have been temperamentally alike, for their correspondence glowed with their mutual exuberance for the allure of the Orient. They were sure that the West had lost touch with age-old insights into the mysteries of the universe.

Thus, by 1925, Jung was restless for more adventure. He especially regretted his inability to speak the local language in his earlier trip to North Africa. And so, with several companions, he traveled to the United States to explore the ancient settlements of the Pueblo people in New Mexico. Having repeatedly visited cities like New York and Chicago, he was now eager for a close look at the original inhabitants of our continent and their way of life.

Jung spent a good deal of time with a Pueblo chief poetically named Ochwiay Bianco (Mountain Lake). He, too, was a middle-aged man. Mountain Lake was quite willing to share his impressions of the Europeans who had conquered his people. But he was rather reticent to speak of his tribe's spiritual beliefs. In a lively exchange, Jung reported:

"See," Ochwiay Bianco said, "how cruel the whites look. Their lips are thin, their noses sharp, their faces furrowed and distorted by folds. Their eyes have a staring expression. . . . The whites always want something; they are always uneasy and restless. We do not know what they want. We do not understand them. We think that they are mad."

I asked him why he thought the whites were all mad. "They say that they think with their heads," he replied. "Why, of course. What do you think with?" I asked him in surprise. "We think here," he said, indicating his heart.[24]

The two men would sit together for hours under the blazing desert sun. Like Carlos Castaneda's Don Juan, Mountain Lake often communicated more through his silences than through his words. For the first time, Jung saw what he called the "real white man" and his bloodthirsty history. Like most of his European colleagues, he had automatically assumed that his culture was superior to all others in its values and practices. He suddenly became aware that his own countrymen had sought to systematically crush the religious and ethical teachings of Mountain Lake's people. More than ever, Jung was convinced that dominant Western civilization—particularly as represented by church and state—was a destructive and morally insensitive force in the world.

Eventually, Mountain Lake revealed to Jung some of the Pueblos' concealed notions. The Indian tribe believed that it was entrusted by God to perform certain Nature rituals to the benefit of all humanity. "If we were to cease practicing our religion," the chief declared, "in ten years the sun would no longer rise. Then it would be night forever."[25]

Jung may have been mistaken in interpreting this statement literally, but he was moved by the simple dignity with which the Indians conducted their lives. Their serenity and sense of cosmic purpose contrasted sharply for him with the frenzy he observed in our own society. Until his death, the Swiss psychiatrist would reminisce fondly about the placid days he had spent on "the rooftop of the world" with the Pueblos.

Later that same eventful year of 1925, Jung traveled to East Africa with several companions. From Kenya and Uganda, they made their way up the Nile to Sudan and Egypt. Jung was fascinated by the Elgonyi tribe, but was unable to gain the trust of its leaders and thus learn something of its spiritual beliefs. He was especially interested in hearing their dreams and comparing them to our own dreams in the West. The Elgonyi, however, refused to cooperate with him. No doubt, to them, the tall European represented the same presence that Jung saw all around—the overbearing, arrogant British colonial government. In fact, under such rule, the Elgonyi were rapidly losing their entire cultural integrity, Jung noticed to his dismay.

In the Sudan, the Swiss psychiatrist participated in an ecstatic dance of a ritual nature. Interestingly, here Jung encountered exuberance that so frightened him, he feared that an orgiastic riot was imminent. He urged the chief to stop the dance immediately. Perhaps this unsettling experience was symbolic on another level, for upon Jung's return to Switzerland he began to search more intensely for spiritual and psychological knowledge in our own civilization's roots.

Carl Jung's last exotic journey came more than a dozen years later in 1938. The British government invited him to serve as a guest speaker at the twenty-fifth anniversary of the University of Calcutta's founding. By that time, he had also practiced yoga at least occasionally since his "confrontation with the unconscious" during World War I.

Jung regarded his trip to India as his first direct experience with an alien, highly literate culture. On this venture, he succeeded in meeting and conversing at length with several Indian *gurus*. He was particularly intrigued by what they might have to say about our inner potential and higher makeup.

In his rather involved discussions with these "holy men," Jung learned that they had little interest in what we would call ordinary disorders. Instead, their goal was "the same as that of Western mysticism, the shifting of the centre of gravity from the ego to the self, from man to God."[26] Jung concluded that they had indeed developed and perfected various techniques to still the conscious ego and awaken the intuitive powers of the psyche. In many ways, the Indian gurus possessed more genuine insight into the working of our world within than did his European and American colleagues, Jung affirmed.

Accompanied by a local priest, he also visited a famous temple in Konarak (Orissa). The walls were covered from base to pinnacle with "exquisitely obscene sculptures," depicting nude couples embracing in multiple positions of lovemaking. The priest assured the astonished Swiss psychiatrist that the lewd spectacle was actually spiritually oriented—for without first experiencing the delights of sexual love we could not pass through its gates into transcendent ecstasies, he explained.

Jung's final impression of India was that despite its alien appearance, this ancient culture had a wealth of knowledge to teach us about the psyche. In his provocative essay, *The Holy Men of India* (1944), he insisted that our breathless, extraverted society was sadly lacking in several key traits espoused by the age-old Oriental spiritual disciplines. "The wisdom and mysticism of the East," he declared, "have therefore very much to say to us, even when they speak their own inimitable language. They serve to remind us that we in our culture possess something similar, which we have already forgotten, and to direct our attention to the fate of the inner man."[27]

## THE SORCERER'S APPRENTICE

When in 1926 Jung returned from his travels to New Mexico and East Africa he was, by his friends' accounts, a visibly changed man. At the age of fifty, he seemed to have indeed undergone an inner transformation. Earlier photograghs present a large, tight-lipped man with small, intense eyes—the figure of a Prussian military officer. Now, he appeared more relaxed, mellow, convivial. In his exotic journeys, he had discovered unmistakable parallels between humanity's ancient myths and the outlook of contemporary non-Western peoples. Clearly, he had found proof of his thesis that we are all united within by a vast collective realm.

And yet, Jung had not really found his own spiritual path. His years of studying Gnosticism had led him into a blind alley, for he was unable to relate early, esoteric Christian thought to twentieth-century problems. Nor could he find much tangible use for the Oriental traditions; their assumptions about the individual and society appeared too alien for adoption by Europeans or Americans.

Then, in 1928, Richard Wilhelm invited Jung to collaborate with him on the publication of *The Secret of the Golden Flower*, a work of Chinese alchemy. The project focused the Swiss thinker's attention once more on Taoism and the *I Ching*, as well as on the Eastern notion of a life energy that flows through *chakras* (vibratory "wheels") in the human body. For the first time, too, Jung was now ready to argue publicly for the importance of the *mandala* as a key symbol of our higher Self—for he had found numerous *mandala* references in this old text. But perhaps most crucially for Jung himself, the collaboration sparked his curiosity in Western alchemy.

Something in the arcane subject attracted Jung. Soon, he had completed reading all the available books on alchemy. His curiosity still piqued, he next began to purchase rare volumes through the services of an antiquarian. Before long, Jung had started to amass one of Europe's largest collections on this abstruse topic.

Initially, the Swiss psychiatrist scarcely knew what he was looking for. The material was vast and bewildering, especially as it was written in Greek and Latin. But the tomes "persistently intrigued" Jung and he slowly but methodically unraveled their complexity. Not unlike an intelligence officer breaking an enemy code, he painstakingly copied down and cross-referenced recurrent phrases until a pattern emerged.

By the mid-1930s, Jung started to share his exciting discovery with disciples and colleagues: namely, that alchemy—far from being simply a superstitious effort to transmute base elements into gold—was actually an esoteric system of psychological and spiritual knowledge. Of course, he had come upon texts by those who had merely sought a pot of riches. But he had uncovered evidence suggesting that the greatest alchemists, like Paracelsus (1493–1541), had been deeply concerned with our inner transformation. For example, they taught their disciples to be honest, devout, and inwardly harmonious before attempting transmutations in the physical world. The alchemists also offered ways to attain a mental state of clarity and balance.

Moreover, Jung found within these rare volumes of medieval thought a vivid symbolism, strikingly similar to the images in his patients' dreams and fantasies. Once again, here was dramatic proof of the timeless nature of our hidden depths.

Beginning in 1936—and continuing for the rest of his life—the Swiss iconoclast produced a steady series of lectures and articles on the relevance of alchemy for the field of modern psychology. He insisted that the study of this admittedly exotic system would give us entrance into a treasure-house of wisdom about the human psyche—particularly how to achieve wholeness or *individuation* by integrating our "feminine" and "masculine" sides.

In 1944, Jung published his first major work on the subject; appropriately entitled *Psychology and Alchemy*, it linked the alchemists to the esoteric side of Christianity. Even before the book appeared in print, he had already plunged into research for his intended magnum opus, *Mysterium Coniunctionis* (the latter an alchemist term for the "union of opposites"). It was eventually completed about a decade later and dealt extensively with the alchemists' quest for inner unity and the sacred Source. Summarizing years of intensive study, Jung asserted in *Mysterium*:

> Today we see how effectively alchemy prepared the ground for the psychology of the unconscious, firstly by leaving behind, in its treasury of symbols, illustrative material of the utmost value. . . . We can see today that the entire alchemical procedure for uniting the opposites . . . could just as well represent the individuation process of a single individual.[28]

About the same time Carl Jung was quietly poring over his alchemy texts, stormy and unsettling events were occurring in Germany. Without doubt, the story of Jung's early ambivalence toward Nazism remains the most ignoble aspect of an otherwise long and illustrious career. At the outset, it must be emphatically stated that Jung was no anti-Semite; occasional charges that still persist have been effectively refuted by his many Jewish students and colleagues, some of whom like Erich Neumann were Zionists and strong in their Jewish identity.

In essence, this is what happened. When Hitler came to power in 1933, the leading psychotherapy journal, *Zentrablatt*, ceased publication. Its editor, Ernst Kretchmer, president of the German General Society for Psychotherapy, resigned in protest from both positions—as the removal of Jews from medicine was among the first Nazi goals. Later that year, Jung agreed to fill the two vacancies; he held the twin posts until 1939. Soon after the eruption of World War II, Nazis placed his name on their blacklist and would have killed him had they decided to invade Switzerland. In fact, Jung went into hiding for a time when the German invasion appeared imminent.

The Swiss psychiatrist's stance during this period can best be described as naively neutral. He flatly refused to expel Jews from the International Society for Psychotherapy and never called for any persecution of the Jewish people. Yet he allowed the German branch of the Society to "Aryanize" itself. He publicly differentiated "Jewish psychology" from that of the Germanic; yet he also publicly praised the Talmud and collaborated with Jewish colleagues on writing projects. By the late 1930s, he was actively helping Jews to flee what he viewed as Germany's mass psychosis.

## BEYOND TIME AND SPACE

Since his youth, Carl Jung had been deeply absorbed by the question of human immortality. As a medical student, he had read avidly on mediumship, mysticism, and parapsychology. In his later visit with William James, these matters were at the forefront of their lively discussion. And while the focus of Jung's career as a busy practicing psychiatrist inevitably drew him to more mundane concerns, he never abandoned his early interest in the topic of life after death. Thus, in 1944, when Jung brushed directly with death—and experienced a series of transcendent visions—the event only accentuated his fascination for this provocative issue.

After breaking his ankle in an icy fall, Jung suffered an embolism, which led to a heart attack. He was sixty-nine years old. For three weeks, he hovered in a semicoma between life and death. Upon recovering, he reported that he had undergone several remarkable visions that now permanently shaped his view on the hidden nature of our psyche.

In the first vision, Carl Jung found himself floating way up in space and able to see the earth as a beautiful blue globe. Then, suddenly, a meteorite loomed near him and he entered what seemed to be a temple with a Hindu guru seated waiting for him. All at once, the Swiss thinker saw his whole life pass with absolute clarity and objectivity. "It was as if I now carried along with me everything I had ever experienced or done, everything that had happened around me."[29] He was about to cross the threshold into an illuminated room where he would meet "all those people to whom I belong in reality."[30] But a king-like messenger resembling his doctor appeared and told Jung he would have to return to earth. Instantly, the entire scene vanished and he was aware of his hospital surroundings.

What is striking about this tale is not only that it closely conforms to popular accounts of the "near-death experience" (e.g., Raymond Moody's *Life After Life*, Kenneth Ring's *Life at Death*, Michael Sabom's *The Near-Death Experience*), but that Jung's subsequent reaction also parallels that of others. For weeks thereafter, he was depressed and angry that he had been forced to rejoin this vale of sorrow and give up the wonders he had barely glimpsed. Philosophically, he became convinced ever after that earthly life is merely "a segment of existence which is enacted in a three-dimensional boxlike universe especially set up for it."[31]

That is, although Jung developed no systematic theory of what happens to the human psyche after physical mortality, he increasingly ascribed to Kabbalistic notions of the soul's immortal journey. He believed that each soul is reborn on this plane until it has accomplished the specific tasks assigned to it. Then, the soul moves on to higher, more dazzling realms. Jung felt, too, that death should be regarded as a sort of wedding between the newly released soul and the heavenly community awaiting it. Citing Jewish mystical teachings in his later writing (Jung became personally acquainted with Gershom Scholem, the leading scholar of the

Kabbalah), he emphasized that we know so little about the mysteries of earthly life that it is futile to speculate too much about far more incomprehensible matters. Better to live the most productive and humane life and let the world-to-come meet us at the proper time, he stressed.

Jung set forth his full musings on this intriguing subject in *Memories, Dreams, and Reflections*. But perhaps he was most vivid in a letter penned several months after the experience. "What happens at death is so unspeakably glorious that our imagination and our feelings do not suffice to form even an approximation of it,"[32] he declared.

Related to Jung's insistence on our ability to transcend time and space was his exciting notion that our lives may pass beyond causality as well. Based on his clinical work with patients over many decades, Jung found that strange coincidences seemed to pile up during times of emotional significance—such as when we are faced with important decisions to make. For example, a woman might be unsure whether to move to another locale—only to discover that her letter carrier had dropped a wrong letter in her mailbox—a letter originating from that particular city. Or a lonely man might dream that he has fallen in love with a beautiful stranger—only to find himself later that day sitting next to an attractive and apparently interested woman. We all have been struck by such coincidences, but Jung suspected that they may reflect some unknown principle in the universe. As early as 1929, he had coined the term *synchronicity* to describe this sort of phenomenon.

Through the 1930s and early 1940s, Jung gave careful thought to this concept. His letters reveal his growing awareness that Eastern mysticism had for centuries understood this phenomenon and connected it to the inexpressible wholeness of the Tao (loosely translated as the divine "Way"). Having found the *I Ching* to offer excellent advice from a *synchronistic* perspective, he incorporated its use into psychotherapy with his patients. He also counseled them to pay special attention to the coincidences in their lives, for he gradually believed that everything in the cosmos is intimately interrelated.

Interestingly, Carl Jung was not unaware of the philosophical implications of modern physics for this entire subject. In fact, he was among the very first Western thinkers to grapple with the larger questions raised by relativity and quantum mechanics. He met with Albert Einstein in Zurich on several occasions when both were young men; it was then that Jung initially became excited by the possible relevance of the new physics for the study of our universe within. Later, in the 1930s, he became close with Wolfgang Pauli, a key founder of quantum theory. Brilliantly anticipating the current interest aroused by this field, in 1938 Jung insisted:

> I would not be surprised if one day we saw a far-reaching agreement between the basic formulations of psychology and physics. I am convinced that if the two sciences pursue their goals with the utmost consistency and right into the ultimate depths of man, they must hit upon a common formula.[33]

In his foreword to the Wilhelm-Baynes edition of the *I Ching* in 1949 and especially in his longer essay in 1952 entitled *Synchronicity: An Acausal Connecting Principle*, Jung emphasized that the new physics heralded a revolution in our understanding of the nature of time, space, and causality. Divinatory works such as the *Book of Changes* might appear absurd, Jung warned, but eventually Western science as well as Oriental mysticism might embrace such phenomena quite readily. "The irrational fullness of life has taught me never to discard anything," he cautioned, "even when it goes against all our theories (so short-lived at best)."[34]

Throughout these provocative writings, Jung in essence argued that some portion of our inner being remains wholly transcendent of physical laws. He was absolutely certain of the reality of psychic phenomena, for he had witnessed too many inexplicable events to remain a sceptic. Indeed, in a letter to J. B. Rhine, the founder of experimental parapsychology, Jung confided that he had personally undergone experiences that he had learned to keep hidden; otherwise, he implied, he might have been recommended to a mental institution himself. Telepathy, precognition, clairvoyance, déjà vu, and uncanny coincidence—all were signs that some unknown force occasionally intervenes in our mundane world, Jung stressed.

The Swiss thinker acknowledged that he had only the barest conjectures to offer as to the nature of this force. And he conceded that he was unable to picture what a higher universe—not based on space, time, or causality—would be like. But Jung regarded such ancient systems as the I Ching and astrology as at least partially tuned into this unknown power. In his last few years, he urged that scientists systematically explore this whole issue. Only then would real answers be forthcoming, he felt.

## THE WISE OLD MAN

In many respects, Carl Jung's last decades of life were his most graceful, charmed period. Surrounded by family, close friends, and loyal disciples, he steadily continued to treat patients and to publish. Decades earlier, he had argued that modern civilization had forgotten the true purpose of aging. "Where is the wisdom of our old people? Where are their precious secrets and their visions? For the most part, our old people try to compete with the young,"[35] he had insisted as a middle-aged man. Now, in his mid-seventies and eighties, he had the courage to follow his own teachings.

When World War II finally ended, the elderly Jung was

suddenly faced with an unprecedented degree of interest in his work. The resumption of normal relations among the nations brought him a voluminous correspondence and a seemingly endless procession of visitors and prospective students. In 1946, a second heart attack convinced him that he could no longer function as a one-man university. Reluctantly, he agreed to set up a formal institute for training and research. Over his objections, his disciples called it the C. G. Jung Institute and drafted him as its first president in 1948. Two years later, upon his retirement due to ill health, his wife Emma assumed the duties.

The next few years witnessed one of Jung's most creatively fertile periods, as he devoted an increasing proportion of his time to writing. Despite his advanced age, his restless intellect roamed in such diverse fields as religion, comparative mythology, political science, and quantum physics. He also offered periodic lectures at the institute and elsewhere, though his fragile health prevented distant travel.

Besides completing a variety of articles on the nature of our psyche, Jung also published several major works at this time. These included *Aion*, *Answer to Job*, and *Synchronicity: An Acausal Connecting Principle*. In 1955 and 1956, the series culminated in the two volumes of *Mysterium Coniunctionis*, which he considered his definitive statement. Throughout these often abstruse writings, the Swiss psychiatrist grappled with religious questions from his own unique perspective. Never ceasing to reject the label of "mystic," he repeatedly insisted that such criticism revealed only the ignorance of his attackers. "If you call me an occultist because I am seriously investigating *religious, mythological, folkloristic*, and *philosophical fantasies* in modern individuals and ancient texts," he satirically remarked, "then you are bound to diagnose Freud *as a sexual pervert* since he is doing likewise with sexual fantasies, and a psychologically inclined criminologist must needs be a gaol-bird."[36]

During the 1950s, Jung also kept a close eye on the tense world situation. In a profound book, *The Undiscovered Self*, he explored the collapse of traditional Western values and the simultaneous appeal of Marxism for Eastern and industrially backward nations. Jung viewed the United States and Russia as locked in an ideological struggle which might take many decades to ease. Though he immensely distrusted the Soviet system, he was almost equally critical of what the American way of life had become: a single-minded huckstering for more and more material goods—with a welfare dole for the poor.

Modern civilization had found nothing to replace the old religious ideals; the Nazi Holocaust was proof for him of the nihilism of our times. Yet he was hopeful that humanity's true spiritual yearnings might lead to a genuine "new age." In an essay on the global sightings of UFOs, he suggested that perhaps we were all looking toward the skies once more for salvation.

In his own life, the deaths of Toni Wolff in 1953 and then his wife Emma in 1955 struck him deeply. He seemed to grow more aware of his precarious health and became somewhat more accessible to the media. In his last few years, he granted several interviews with radio, film, and the press. Typically, though, he found the level of the questions posed to him quite disappointing and even ludicrous. In response to an invitation by *Esquire* magazine to predict "the most dramatic events of the coming decade," Jung tersely replied, "Being a scientist I prefer not to be a prophet if I can help it. I am in no position to ascertain facts of the future."[37] Fortunately, he finally agreed to publish his autobiography, and with the assistance of his personal secretary Aniela Jaffé, he issued *Memories, Dreams, and Reflections*.

As late as a year before his death, Jung suddenly became excited by a new project, a popular anthology to be entitled *Man and his Symbols*. He busily began preparing a chapter that would distill his lifetime's work on this vast subject. And all through his old age, the Swiss thinker strove to keep up with his voluminous correspondence.

From all over the globe, people in every walk of life wrote to him. They requested his views on mysticism and religion, world events and psychology, and even their own personal problems. His correspondents ranged from famous theologians and therapists to those who were obviously unbalanced. But Jung patiently answered them all. His letters often reveal a puckish, witty temperament difficult to discern in his massively erudite books. He could also be quite poetic. To the Swiss ambassador to Austria, he wrote, "A man's lifework is like a ship he has built and equipped himself, launched down the ramp and entrusted to the sea . . . What remains is what has been."[38]

In 1961, Carl Gustav Jung died quietly after a protracted illness. He was nearly eighty-six years old. On the day of his death, several *synchronistic* events apparently took place. In particular, his favorite garden tree was struck by lightning. The bark was stripped off, but the tree was not destroyed. No doubt Jung, who regarded trees as humanity's timeless symbols of life, would have been pleased by the coincidence.

## NOTES

1. Jung, Carl G. *Memories, Dreams, Reflections*. Recorded and edited by Aniela Jaffé. Translated by Richard and Clara Winston. New York: Random House, 1963, p. 91.

2. Ibid., p. 48.

3. Ibid., p. 75.

4. Ibid., p. 114.

5. *The Freud/Jung Letters: The Correspondence Between Sigmund Freud and C. G. Jung*. Edited by William McGuire. Translated by Ralph Manheim and R. F. C. Hull. Princeton: Princeton University Press, 1974, p. 3.

6. *Memories*, p. 149.

7. Ibid., p. 361.

8. Ibid., p. 8.

9. Jung, *Memories*, p. 150.

10. Gay, Peter. *Freud: A Life for Our Time*. New York: Norton, p. 235.

11. *Memories*, p. 199.

12. Ibid., p. 173.

13. Ibid., p. 191.

14. Jung, *Analytical Psychology*, p. 192.

15. Ibid., p. 46.

16. Op. cit.

17. Jung, *Memories*, p. 207.

18. Op. cit.

19. Jung, *Analytical Psychology*, p. 19.

20. Jung, *Memories*, p. 371.

21. Ibid., p. 372.

22. Ibid., p. 239

23. Ibid., p. 240.

24. Ibid., pp. 247–48.

25. Ibid., p. 252.

26. Jung, *Letters*, vol. 2, p. 217.

26. Jung, C. G. "The Holy Men of India," *Collected Works*. Princeton: Princeton University Press, 1958, vol. 11, p. 581.

27. Ibid., pp. 585–86.

28. Jung, C. G. *Mysterium Coniunctionis, Collected Works*, 1970, p. 21.

29. Jung, *Memories*, p. 291.

30. Op. Cit.

31. Jung, *Memories*, p. 264.

32. Jung, *Letters*, vol. 1, p. 343.

33. Ibid., p. 246.

34. Jung, C. G. "Foreword to the *I Ching*," *Collected Works*, vol. 11, p. xxiv.

35. Jung, "The Stages of Life," *Collected Works*, vol. 8, p. 110.

36. Jung, *Letters*, vol. 2, p. 187.

37. Ibid., p. 513.

38. Ibid., p. 577.

# Part II

**SELECTED WRITINGS**

# JUNG'S VIEW OF HIS OWN WORK

I can only hope and wish that no one becomes "Jungian." I stand for no doctrine, but describe facts and put forward certain views which I hold worthy of discussion. I criticize Freudian psychology for a certain narrowness and bias, and the Freudians for a certain rigid, sectarian spirit of intolerance and fanaticism. I proclaim no cut-and-dried doctrine and I abhor "blind adherents." I leave everyone free to deal with the facts in his own way, since I also claim freedom for myself. (3)

The long path I have traversed is littered with husks sloughed off, witnesses of countless moultings, those *relicta* one calls books. They conceal as much as they reveal. Every step is a symbol of those to follow. He who mounts a flight of steps does not linger on them, nor look back at them, even though age invites him to linger or slow his pace. His gaze sweeps distances that flee away into the infinite. The last steps are the loveliest and most precious, for they lead to that fullness to which the innermost essence of man is born. (3)

Anyone who says that I am a mystic is just an idiot. He just doesn't understand the first word of psychology. (1)

I pursue a scientific psychology which could be called a comparative anatomy of the psyche. I postulate the psyche as something real. (3)

It really is very distressing that the majority of educated people today eschew talk of religious matters. I hold theologians responsible for this up to a point, because they obstinately refuse to admit that they, as much as the rest of us, are talking of anthropomorphic ideas about which we do not know how exactly or inexactly they depict a possible metaphysical fact. In this way, they slaughter every discussion from the start, so that one is obliged to avoid, politely, any conversation with theologians, *very much to the detriment of religious life!*

In my practice, I often had to give elementary school lessons in the history of religion in order to eliminate, for a start, the disgust and nausea people felt for religious matters, who had dealt all their lives only with confession-mongers and preachers. The man of today wants to understand and not be preached at. (3)

I define myself as an empiricist, for after all I have to be something respectable. You yourself admit that I am a poor philosopher, and naturally I don't like being something inferior. As an empiricist, I have at least accomplished something. If a man is a good shoemaker and knows he is one, people will not inscribe on his tombstone that he was a bad hatmaker because he once made an unsatisfactory hat.

I am, more specifically, simply a psychiatrist, for my essential problem, to which all my efforts are directed, is psychic disturbance. Everything else is secondary for me. I do not feel called upon to found a religion, nor to proclaim my belief in one. I am not engaged in philosophy, but merely in thinking within the framework of the special task that is laid upon me: to be a proper psychiatrist, a healer of the soul. This is what I have discovered myself to be, and this is how I function as a member of society. (3)

I have no idea what God is in himself. In my experience, there are only psychic phenomena which are ultimately of unknown origin, since the psyche itself is hopelessly unconscious. My critics all ignore the epistemological barrier which is expressly respected by me. Just as everything we perceive is a psychic phenomena and therefore secondary, so is all inner experience. We should therefore be truly modest and not imagine we can say anything about God himself. (3)

I don't know if it is permissible, in our incompetence, to think on things divine. I find that all my thoughts circle round God like the planets around the sun, and are irresistibly attracted to him. I would feel it is the most heinous sin were I to offer any resistance to this compelling force. I feel it is God's will that I should exercise the gift of thinking that has been vouchsafed me. Therefore I put my thinking at his service. (3)

I cannot force people to take my work seriously, and I cannot persuade them to study it really. The trouble is that I don't construct theories one can learn by heart. I collect facts which are not yet generally known or properly appreciated, and I gave names to observations and experiences unfamiliar to the contemporary mind and objectionable to its prejudices.

Thus, my chief contribution to the further development of the psychology of the unconscious, inaugurated by Freud, suffers from the considerable disadvantage that the doctors interested in psychotherapy have practically no knowledge of the general human mind as it expresses itself in history, archeology, philology, philosophy, and theology.

It is the smallest part of the psyche, and in particular of the unconscious, that presents itself in the medical consulting room. On the other hand, the specialists of the said disciplines are far from any psychological or psychopathological knowledge, and the general public is blissfully unaware of all medical as well as any other kind of real and well-founded knowledge.

The topics under discussion are of a highly complex nature. How can I popularize things so difficult, and demanding such an unusual amount of specific knowledge, to a public that does not or cannot take the trouble to settle down to a careful study of the facts collected in many volumes? How can anyone express the essentials of modern physics in two words? (3)

For your orientation, I am a psychiatrist and not a philosopher: merely an empiricist who ponders on certain experiences. (3)

Thank you for your kind letter. You are the first representative of the Japanese nation from whom I hear that he has read my books. So your letter is a memorable fact in my life. It shows how slow mental traveling is: it took me more than thirty years to reach Japan, but I have not even arrived yet at the university in my own town.

It is indeed most gratifying and encouraging for me to know that I have readers in Japan, since I know how specifically European most of my works are. It is true, however, that I have tried to demonstrate the universal character of the psyche as well as I could. But it is almost a superhuman task. "Art is long, life is short." I am now in my 83rd year, and my creative work has come to an end. I am watching the setting sun. (3)

Unfortunately, I'm unable to interpret your dream. I wouldn't dare to let my intuitions handle your material. But, since I appear in your dream, I cannot refrain from making the remark that I like thick walls, and I like trees and green things, and I like many books. Perhaps you are in need of these three good things. (3)

Being a scientist, I prefer not to be a prophet if I can help it. I am in no position to ascertain facts of the future. (3)

When I examined the course of development in patients who quietly, as if unconsciously, outgrew [their former] selves, I saw that their fates had something in common. The new thing came to them from obscure possibilities, either outside or inside themselves; they accepted it and grew with its help.

It seemed to me typical that some took the new thing from outside themselves, others from inside; or rather, that it grew into some persons from without, and into others from within.

But the new thing never came exclusively from within or without. If it came from outside, it became a profound inner experience; if it came from inside, it became an outer happening. In no case was it conjured into existence intentionally or by conscious willing, but rather seemed to be borne along on the stream of time. (84)

I have no theory about dreams, I do not know how dreams arise. And I am not at all sure that my way of handling dreams even deserves the name of a "method." I share all your prejudices against dream-interpretation as the quintessence of uncertainty and arbitrariness.

On the other hand, I know that if we meditate on a dream sufficiently long and thoroughly, if we carry it around with us and turn it over and over, something almost always comes of it. This something is not, of course, a scientific result to be boasted about or rationalized; but it is an important practical hint which shows the patient what the unconscious is aiming at. Indeed, it ought not to matter to me whether the result of my musings on the dream is scientifically verifiable or tenable; otherwise, I am pursuing an ulterior—and autoerotic—aim.

I must content myself wholly with the fact that the result means something to the patient and sets his life in motion again. I may allow myself only one criterion for the result of my labors: does it work? As for my scientific hobby—my desire to know *why* it works—this I must reserve for my spare time. (13)

When the famous Einstein was Professor at Zurich, I often saw him, and it was when he was beginning to work on his theory of relativity. He was often in my house, and I pumped him about his relativity theory. I am not gifted in mathematics, and you should have seen all the trouble the poor man had to explain relativity to me. He did not know how to do it. I went fourteen feet deep into the floor and felt quite small when I saw how he was troubled.

But one day, he asked me something about psychology. Then I had my revenge. (4)

I have no power complex in the [Adlerian] sense because I have been fairly successful and in nearly every respect I have been able to adapt. If the whole world disagrees with me, it is perfectly indifferent to me. I have a perfectly good place in Switzerland, I enjoy myself, and if nobody enjoys my books, I enjoy them. I know nothing better than being in my library, and if I make discoveries in my books, that is wonderful.

I cannot say I have a Freudian psychology because I never had such difficulties in relation to desires. As a boy, I lived in the country and took things very naturally, and the natural and unnatural things of which Freud speaks were not interesting to me. To talk of an incest complex just bores me to tears. (4)

I could never bring myself to be frightfully interested in these sex cases [like Freud]. They do exist, there are people with a neurotic sex life, and you have to talk sex stuff with them until they get sick of it, and you get out of that boredom. Naturally, with my temperamental attitude, I hope to goodness we shall get through with the stuff as quickly as possible. It is neurotic stuff, and no reasonable normal person talks of it for any length of time. Many people make unnecessary difficulties about sex when their actual troubles are of quite a different nature. (4)

Old age is only half as funny as one is inclined to think. It is at all events the gradual breaking down of the bodily machine, with which foolishness identifies ourselves. It is indeed a major effort—the *magnum opus*, in fact—to escape in time from the narrowness of its embrace and to liberate our mind to the vision of the immensity of the world, of which we form an infinitesimal part. In spite of the enormity of our scientific cognition, we are yet hardly at the bottom of the ladder, but we are at least so far that we are able to recognize the smallness of our knowledge.

The older I grow, the more impressed I am by the frailty

and uncertainty of our understanding, and all the more I take recourse to the simplicity of immediate experience so as not to lose contact with the essentials: namely, the dominants which rule human existence throughout the millenniums. (3)

# UNDERSTANDING THE HUMAN PSYCHE

Man cannot compare himself with any other creature. He is not a monkey, not a cow, not a tree. I am a man. But what is it to be that? Like every other human being, I am a splinter of the infinite deity, but I cannot contrast myself with any animal, any plant, or any stone. Only a mythical being has a range greater than man's. How then can a man form any definite opinions about himself? (6)

If the human [soul] is anything, it must be of unimaginable complexity and diversity, so that it cannot possibly be approached through a mere psychology of instinct. I can only gaze with wonder and awe at the depths and heights of our psychic nature. Its non-spatial universe conceals an untold abundance of images which have accumulated over millions of years of living development and become fixed in the organism.

My consciousness is like an eye that penetrates to the most distant spaces, yet it is the psychic non-ego that fills them with non-spatial images. And these images are not pale shadows, but tremendously powerful psychic factors . . .

Beside this picture, I would like to place the spectacle of the starry heavens at night, for the only equivalent of the universe within is the universe without; and just as I reach this world through the medium of the body, so I reach that world through the medium of the psyche. (6)

The psyche is by no means *tabula rasa,* but a definite mixture and combination of genes, which are there from the very first moment of our life; and they give a definite character, even to the little child. (1)

Do we ever understand what we think? We only understand that kind of thinking which is a mere question, from which nothing comes out but what we have put in. That is the working of the intellect. But besides that there is a thinking in primordial images, in symbols which are older than the historical man, which are inborn in him from the earliest times, and, eternally living, outlasting all generations, still make up the groundwork of the human psyche. It is only possible to live the fullest life when we are in harmony with these symbols; wisdom is a return to them. (74)

It is a remarkable fact, which we have come across again and again, that absolutely everybody, even the most unqualified layman, thinks he knows all about psychology as though the psyche were something that enjoyed the most universal understanding. But anybody who really knows the human psyche will agree with me when I say that it is one of the darkest and most mysterious regions of our experience. There is no end to what can be learned in this field. (58)

There are two sciences in our days which are at immediate grips with the basic problems: nuclear physics and the psychology of the unconscious. There things begin to look really tough, as those who have an inkling of understanding of the one thing are singularly incapable of grasping the other thing: and here, so it looks, the great confusion of languages begins, which once already has destroyed a tower of Babel.

I am trying to hold those two worlds together as long as my [bodily] machinery allows the effort, but it seems to be a condition which is desperately similar to that of the political world, the solution of which nobody yet can foresee. It is quite possible that we look at the world from the wrong side and that we might find the right answer by changing our point of view and looking at it from the other side: that is, not from outside, but from inside. (3)

Every science is a function of the psyche, and all knowledge is rooted in it. The psyche is the greatest of all cosmic wonders. (44)

The psychological investigator is always finding himself obliged to make extensive use of an indirect method of description in order to present the reality he has observed. Only in so far as elementary facts are communicated which are amenable to quantitative measurement can there be any question of a direct presentation. But how much of the actual psychology of man can be experienced and observed as quantitatively measurable facts? (56)

Every other science has, so to speak, an outside; not so psychology, whose object is the inside subject of all science. (44)

Theories in psychology are the very devil. It is true that we need certain viewpoints for their orienting and heuristic value. But they should always be regarded as mere auxiliary concepts that can be laid aside at any time.

We still know so very little about the psyche that it is positively grotesque to think we are far enough advanced to frame general theories. We have not even established the empirical extent of the psyche's phenomenology: how then can we dream of general theories? No doubt, theory is the best cloak for lack of experience and ignorance, but the consequences are depressing: bigotry, superficiality, and scientific sectarianism. (52)

You can learn a great deal of psychology through studying books, but you will find that this psychology is not very helpful in practical life. A [person] entrusted with the care of souls ought to have a certain wisdom of life which does not consist of words only, but chiefly of experience. Such psychology, as I understand it, is not only a piece of knowledge, but a certain wisdom of life at the same time. If such a thing can be taught at all, it must be in the way of a personal experience of the human soul. Such an experience is possible only when the teaching has a personal character, namely when you are personally taught and not generally. (3)

It always amuses me when people say they dismiss psychology. It would never occur to me to dismiss literary studies or aesthetics because they are too concerned with certain aspects of the human psyche, and I can never understand with what justification my colleagues in other professional fields can dismiss psychology out of hand. I would never dream of putting psychology in the place of aesthetics or the like.

On the other hand, it is obvious to every child that the artist has a human psyche whose qualities are at least similar to those of ordinary mortals. I understand the resistance better in the case of philosophers, since psychology saws off the branch they are sitting on by wickedly robbing them of the illusion that they represent the absolute spirit. (3)

The nature of the psyche reaches into obscurities far beyond the scope of our understanding. It contains as many riddles as the universe with its galactic systems, before whose majestic configurations only a mind lacking in imagination can fail to admit its own insufficiency. This extreme uncertainty of human comprehension makes the intellectualistic hubbub not only ridiculous, but also deplorably dull. (72)

All psychic events are so deeply grounded in the archetype and are so much interwoven with it that in every case considerable critical effort is needed to separate the unique from the typical with any certainty. Ultimately, every individual life is at the same time the eternal life of the species. The individual is continuously "historical" because strictly time-bound; the relation of the type to time, on the other hand, is irrelevant. . . . Since the archetype is the unconscious precondition of every human life, its life, when revealed, also reveals the hidden, unconscious ground-life of every individual. (60)

A symbol loses its magical or, if you prefer, its redeeming power as soon as its liability to dissolve is recognized. To be effective, a symbol must be by its very nature unassailable. It must be the best possible expression of the prevailing worldview, an unsurpassed container of meaning; it must also be sufficiently remote from comprehension to resist all attempts of the critical intellect to break it down; and finally, its aesthetic form must appeal so convincingly to our feelings that no arguments can be raised against it on that score. (56)

Not for a moment dare we succumb to the illusion that an archetype can be finally explained and disposed of. Even the best attempts at explanation are only more or less successful translations into another metaphorical language. (Indeed, language itself is only an image.) The most we can do is to *dream the myth onwards* and give it a modern dress. And whatever explanation or interpretation does to it, we do to our own souls as well, with corresponding results for our own well-being. The archetype—let us never forget this—is a psychic organ present in all of us. (62)

The soul gives birth to images that from the rational standpoint of consciousness are assumed to be worthless. And so they are, in the sense that they cannot immediately be turned to account in the objective world. The first possibility of making use of them is artistic, if one is in any way gifted in that direction; a second is philosophical speculation; a third is quasi-religious, leading to heresy and the founding of sects; and a fourth way of employing the *dynamis* of these images is to squander it in every form of licentiousness. (56)

I can only gaze with wonder and awe at the depths and heights of our psychic nature. Its non-spatial universe conceals an untold abundance of images which have accumulated over millions of years of living development and become fixed in the organism. My consciousness is like an eye that penetrates to the most distant spaces, yet it is the psychic non-ego that fills them with non-spatial images. And these images are not pale shadows, but tremendously powerful psychic factors.

The most we may be able to do is misunderstand them, but we can never rob them of their power by denying them. Beside this picture, I would like to place the spectacle of the starry heavens at night, for the only equivalent of the universe within is the universe without; and just as I reach this world through the medium of the body, so I reach that world through the medium of the psyche. (60)

The so-called "forces of the unconscious" are not intellectual concepts that can be arbitrarily manipulated, but dangerous antagonists which can, among other things, work frightful devastation in the economy of the personality. They are everything one could wish for or fear in a psychic "Thou." The layman naturally thinks he is the victim of some obscure organic disease; but the theologian, who suspects it is the devil's work, is apparently nearer to the psychological truth. (69)

Many people flatly deny the existence of the unconscious, or else they say that it consists merely of instincts, or of repressed or forgotten contents that were once part of the conscious mind. It is safe to assume that what the East calls "mind" has more to do with our "unconscious" than with mind as we understand it, which is more-or-less identical with consciousness.

To us, consciousness is inconceivable without an ego; it is equated with the relation of contents to an ego. If there is no ego, there is nobody to be conscious of anything. The ego is therefore indispensable to the conscious process. The Eastern mind, however, has no difficulty in conceiving of a consciousness without an ego. Consciousness is deemed capable of transcending its ego condition; indeed, in its "higher" forms, the ego disappears altogether. (28)

The psyche and its structure are real enough. They even transform material objects into psychic images. They do not perceive waves, but sound; not wave-lengths, but colors. Existence is as we see and understand it. There are innumerable things that can be seen, felt, and understood in a great variety of ways.

Quite apart from merely personal prejudices, the psyche assimilates external facts in its own way, which is based ultimately upon the laws of pattern of apperception. These laws do not change, although different ages or different parts of the world call them by different names.

On a primitive level, people are afraid of witches; on the modern level, we are apprehensively aware of microbes. There everybody believes in ghosts, here everybody believes in vitamins. (28)

In spite of the fact that the majority of people do not know why the body needs salt, everyone demands it nonetheless because of an instinctive need. It is the same with the things of the psyche. (74)

Besides the intellect [we each have] symbols, which are older than the historical man, which are inborn in him from the earliest times, and, eternally living, outlasting all generations, still make up the groundwork of the human psyche. It is only possible to live fullest life when we are in harmony with these symbols. Wisdom is a return to them. . . . They are the unthinkable matrices of all our thoughts, no matter what our conscious mind may cogitate. (74)

Just as the "psychic infra-red," the biological instinctual psyche, gradually passes into the physiology of the organism and merges with its chemical and physical conditions, so the "psychic ultra-violet," the archetype, describes a field which exhibits none of the peculiarities of the physiological and yet, in the last analysis, can no longer be regarded as psychic. (44)

I have often been asked where the archetype comes from and whether it is acquired or not. This question cannot be answered directly. Archetypes are, by definition, factors and motifs that arrange the psychic elements into certain images, characterized as archetypal, but in such a way that they can be recognized only from the effects they produce. They exist preconsciously, and presumably they form the structural dominants of the psyche in general. They may be compared to the invisible presence of the crystal lattice in a saturated solution.

As *a priori* conditioning factors, they represent a special, psychological instance of the biological "pattern of behavior," which gives all living organisms their specific qualities. Just as the manifestations of this biological ground plan may change in the course of development, so also can those of the archetype. Empirically considered, however, the archetype did not ever come into existence as a phenomenon of organic life, but entered into the picture with life itself. (53)

Sooner or later, nuclear physics and the psychology of the unconscious will draw close together as both of them, independently of one another and from opposite directions, push forward into transcendental territory, the one with the concept of the atom, the other with that of the archetype. (14)

Without consciousness there would, practically speaking, be no world, for the world exists for us only in so far as it is consciously reflected by a psyche. Consciousness is a precondition of being. Thus, the psyche is endowed with the dignity of a cosmic principle, which philosophically and in fact gives it a position co-equal with the principle of physical being.

The carrier of this consciousness is the individual, who does not produce the psyche of his own volition but is, on the contrary, preformed by it and nourished by the gradual awakening of consciousness during childhood. If therefore the psyche is of overriding empirical importance, so also is the individual, who is the only immediate manifestation of the psyche. (82)

What is an "illusion"? By what criteria do we judge something to be an illusion? Does anything exist for the psyche that we are entitled to call illusion? What we are pleased to call illusion may be for the psyche an extremely important life-factor, something as indispensable as oxygen for the body—a psychic actuality of overwhelming significance.

Presumably the psyche does not trouble itself about our categories of reality; for it, everything that *works* is real. The investigator of the psyche must confuse it with his consciousness, else he veils from his sight the object of his investigation. On the contrary, to recognize it at all, he must learn to see how different it is from consciousness. Nothing is more probable than that which we call illusion is very real for the psyche—for which reason we cannot take psychic reality to be commensurable with conscious reality. (13)

Far from being a material world, this is a psychic world, which allows us to make only indirect and hypothetical inferences about the real nature of matter. The psychic alone has immediate reality, and this includes all forms of the psychic, even "unreal" ideas and thoughts which refer to nothing "external." We may call them "imagination" or "delusion," but that does not detract in any way from their effectiveness. Indeed, there is no "real" thought that cannot, at times, be thrust aside by an "unreal" one, thus proving that the latter is stronger and more effective than the former.

Greater than all physical dangers are the tremendous effects of delusional ideas, which are yet denied all reality by our world-blinded consciousness. Our much vaunted reason and our boundlessly overestimated will are sometimes utterly powerless in the face of "unreal" thoughts. The world powers that rule over all humanity, for good or ill, are unconscious psychic factors, and it is they that bring unconsciousness into being and hence create the *sine qua non* for the existence of any world at all. We are steeped in a world that was created by our own psyche. (67)

Every science is descriptive at the point where it can no longer proceed experimentally, without on that account ceasing to be scientific. But an experimental science makes itself impossible when it delimits its field of work in accordance with theoretical concepts. The psyche does not come to an end where some physiological assumption or other stops. In other words, in each individual case that we observe scientifically, we have to consider the manifestations of the psyche in their totality. (97)

Metaphysical assertions are statements of the psyche, and are therefore psychological. To the Western mind, which compensates its well-known feelings of resentment by a slavish regard for "rational" explanations, this obvious truth seems all too obvious, or else it is seen as an inadmissible negation of all metaphysical "truth."

Whenever the Westerner hears the word "psychological," it always sounds to him like "*only* psychological." For him, the "soul" is something pitifully small, unworthy, personal, subjective, and a lot more besides. He therefore prefers to use the word "mind" instead, though he likes to pretend at the same time that a statement which may be very subjective indeed is made by the "mind," naturally by the "Universal Mind," or even—at a pinch—by the "Absolute" itself. This rather ridiculous presumption is probably a compensation for the regrettable smallness of the soul. (27)

I do not underestimate the psyche in any respect whatsoever, nor do I imagine for a moment that psychic happenings vanish into thin air by being explained. Psychologisms represent a still primitive mode of magical thinking, with the help of which one hopes to conjure the reality of the soul out of existence. (17)

At a time when all available energy is spent in the investigation of nature, very little attention is paid to the essence of man, which is his psyche, although many researches are made into its conscious functions. But the really unknown part, which produces symbols, is still virtually unexplored. We receive signals from it every night, yet deciphering these communications seems to be such an odious task that very few people in the whole civilized world can be bothered with it. Man's greatest instrument, his psyche, is little thought of, if not actually mistrusted and despised. "It's only psychological" too often means: it's nothing. (5)

The psyche does not merely *react*, it gives its own specific answer to the influences at work upon it, and at least half the resulting formation is entirely due to the psyche and the determinants inherent within it. That shallow explanation can safely be left to the past century. It is just these determinants that appear as psychological imperatives, and we have daily proof of their compelling power. What I call "biological duty" is identical with these determinants. (71)

What more natural conclusion can we draw than that we are dealing here with a generally human disposition, which is instinctive and innate, as instinct is with all animals? How else can we explain identical or analogous products among tribes and individuals who could not have known of the existence of parallel creations? Do you really believe that every chick invents its own way of breaking out of the egg? Or that every eel makes an individual decision to start for the Bermudas, as though the idea were entirely novel? (3)

The Oedipus complex is what I call an archetype. That is the first archetype that Freud discovered; the first and only one. He thought that this *was* the archetype. You look at Greek mythology and you find them, any amount of them. Or look at dreams and you find any amount of them. To Freud, however, incest was so impressive that he chose the term "Oedipus complex," because that was one of the outstanding examples of an incest complex; though, mind you, it is only in masculine form, because women have an incest complex too. . . .

Oedipus gives you an excellent example of the behavior of an archetype. It is always a whole situation. There is a mother, a father, a son; so there is a whole story of how such a situation develops and to what end it leads finally. That is an archetype. (1)

An archetype always is a sort of abbreviated drama. It begins in such and such a way, it extends to such and such a complication, and finds its solution in such and such a way. That is the usual form. For instance, take the instinct in birds of building their nests. In the way they build the nest, there is the beginning, the middle, and the end. The nest is built just to suffice for a certain number of young. The end is already anticipated. That is the reason why, in the archetype itself, there is no time; it is a timeless condition where beginning, middle, and end are just the same. They are all given in one. That is only a hint to what the archetype can do. (1)

I began to see that the structure of what I then called the "collective unconscious" was really a sort of agglomeration of [powerful] images, each of which had a numinous quality.

The archetypes are, at the same time, dynamic. They are instinctual images that are not intellectually invented. They are always there and they produce certain processes in the unconscious that could best be compared with myths. That's the origin of mythology. Mythology is a pronouncing of a series of images that formulate the life of archetypes. (1)

You see, the archetype is a force. It has autonomy, and it can suddenly seize you. It is like a seizure. So, for instance, is falling in love at first sight, that is such a case. You have a certain image in yourself, without knowing it, of the woman—of *the* woman. You see that girl, or at least a good imitation of your type, and instantly, you get the seizure and you are gone. And afterward you may discover that it was a hell of a mistake.

You see, a man is quite capable, or is intelligent enough to see that the woman of his choice was no choice; he has been captured. He sees that she is no good at all and says, "For God's sake, doctor, help me to get rid of that woman." He can't though, and he is like clay in her fingers. That is the archetype. (1)

The *persona* is a practical concept we need in elucidating people's relations. I noticed with my patients, particularly with people that are in public life, that they have a certain way of presenting themselves. For instance, take a doctor. He has a certain way; he has good bedside manners, and he behaves as one expects a doctor to behave. He may even identify himself with it, and believe he is what he appears to be. He must appear in a certain form, or else people won't believe that he is a doctor. And so when one is a professor, he is also supposed to behave in a certain way so that it is plausible that he is a professor. So the *persona* is partially the result of the demands society has.

On the other side, it is a compromise with what one likes to be, or one likes to appear. Take, for instance, a parson. He also has his particular manner and, of course, runs into the general societal expectations; but he behaves also in another way, combined with his *persona* that is forced upon him by society in such a way that his fiction of himself, his idea about himself, is more or less portrayed or represented.

So the *persona* is a certain complicated system of behavior which is partially dictated by society and partially dictated by the expectations or the wishes one nurses himself. Now this is not the real personality. In spite of the fact that people will assure you that it is all quite real and quite honest, yet it is not.

Such a performance of the *persona* is quite all right, as long as you know that you are not identical to the way in which you appear: but if you are unconscious of this fact, then you get into sometimes very disagreeable conflicts.

Namely, people can't help noticing that at home you are quite different from what you appear to be in public. People who don't know it stumble over it in the end. They deny that they *are* like that; they are it. Then you don't know—now which is the real man? Is he the man as he is at home or in intimate relations, or is he the man that appears in public? (1)

There are people who have an amazing knowledge of themselves, of the things that go on in themselves. But even those people wouldn't be capable of knowing what is going on in their unconscious. For instance, they are not conscious of the fact that while they live a conscious life, all the time a myth is played in the unconscious, a myth that extends over centuries: namely, a stream of archetypal ideas that goes on through an individual through the centuries. Really, it is like a continuous stream, one that comes into the daylight in the great movements, say, in political or spiritual movements. For instance, in the time before the Reformation, people dreamed of the great change. That is the reason why such great transformations could be predicted.

If somebody is clever enough to see what is going on in people's minds, in the unconscious mind, he will be able to predict. For instance, I could have predicted the Nazi rising in Germany through the observation of my German patients. They had dreams in which the whole thing was anticipated, and with considerable detail. And I was absolutely certain—in the years before Hitler, before Hitler came in the beginning; I could say the year, 1919, I was sure that something was threatening in Germany, something very big, very catastrophic. I only knew it through the observation of the unconscious. (1)

The *self* is merely a term that designates the whole personality. The whole personality of man is indescribable. His consciousness can be described; his unconscious cannot be described, because the unconscious—and I repeat myself—is always unconscious. It is really unconscious; he really does not know it. And so we don't know our unconscious personality. We have hints and certain ideas, but we don't know it really.

Nobody can say where man ends. That is the beauty of it, you know. It is very interesting. The unconscious of man can reach . . . God knows where. There we are going to make discoveries. (1)

The *mandala* is an age-old archetypal symbol that goes right back to the prehistory of man. It is all over the earth, and it either expresses the Deity or the self; and these two terms are psychologically very much related, which doesn't mean that I believe that God is the self or that the self is God. I made the statement that there is a psychological relation [for belief in God], and there is plenty of evidence for that.

It is a very important archetype. It is the archetype of inner order, and it is always used in that sense, either to make arrangements of the many, many aspects of the universe—a world scheme—or to arrange the complicated aspects of our psyche into a scheme. It expresses the fact that there is a center and a periphery, and it tries to embrace the whole. It is the symbol of wholeness. . . .

A *mandala* spontaneously appears as a compensatory archetype during times of disorder. It appears, bringing order, showing the possibility of order and centeredness. It means a center which is not coincident with the ego, but with the wholeness—which I call the "self": this is the term for wholeness. I am not whole in my ego, as my ego is but a fragment of my personality. . . . The mandala is highly important and highly autonomous, a symbol that appears in dreams and in folklore. We could say that it is the main archetype. (1)

The intuitive type is very little understood, but has a very important function, because he is going by hunches. He sees around corners. He smells a rat a mile away. He can give you perception and orientation in a situation where your senses, your intellect, and your feelings are no good at all. When you are in an absolute fix, an intuition can show you the hole through which you can escape. This is a very important function under primitive conditions or wherever you are confronted with vital issues that you cannot master by rules or logic. (1)

The shadow personifies everything that the subject refuses to acknowledge about himself and yet is always thrusting itself upon him directly or indirectly: for instance, inferior traits of character and other incompatible tendencies. (6)

The shadow is that hidden, repressed, for the most part inferior and guilt-laden personality whose ultimate ramifications reach back into the realm of our animal ancestors and so comprise the whole historical aspect of the unconscious. . . . If it has been believed hitherto that the human shadow was the source of all evil, it can now be ascertained on closer investigation that the unconscious man, that is, his shadow, does not consist only of morally reprehensible tendencies, but also displays a number of good qualities, such as animal instincts, appropriate reactions, realistic insights, and creative impulses. (6)

It is quite in order that your boy should have a mandala dream. Such dreams occur normally and not too infrequently between the ages of 4 and 6. The mandala is an archetype that is always present, and children, who are not yet spoiled, have a clearer vision for divine things than adults, whose understanding is already ruined. The mandala should really have four colors to be complete. The reason for the absence of the fourth color may be either that he is already going to school, or that he is the son of a teacher who has an instinctive interest in the differentiation of the functions.

Nowadays, animals, dragons, and other living creatures are readily replaced in dreams by railways, locomotives, motorcycles, airplanes, and such like artificial objects—just as the starry sky in the southern hemisphere, discovered relatively late by European navigators, contains many nautical images.

This expresses the remoteness of the modern mind from nature; animals have lost their numinosity. They have become apparently harmless; instead we people the world with hooting, booming, clattering monsters that cause infinitely more damage to life and limb than bears and wolves ever did in the past. And where the natural dangers are lacking, man does not rest until he has immediately invented others for himself. (3)

Nobody has ever seen an archetype, and nobody has ever seen an atom either. But the former is known to produce numinous effects and the latter, explosions. When I say "atom" I am talking of ideas corresponding to it, but never of the thing-in-itself, which in both cases is a transcendental mystery. It would never occur to a physicist that he has bagged the bird with his atomic model. He is fully aware that he is handling a variable schema which merely points to unknowable facts. (3)

The ego receives the light from the self. Though we know of the self, it is not known. You may see a big town and know its name and geographical position, yet you do not know a single one of its inhabitants. You may even know a man through daily intercourse, yet you can be entirely ignorant of his real character. The ego is contained in the self as it is contained in the universe of which we know only the tiniest section. (3)

The "archetype" is practically synonymous with the biological concept of the behavior pattern. But as the latter designates external phenomena chiefly, I have chosen the term "archetype" for "psychic patterns." We don't know whether the weaver-bird beholds a mental image while it follows an immemorial and inherited model in building its nest, but there is no doubt that no weaver-bird in our experience has ever invented its nest. It is as if the image of nest building were born with the bird.

As no animal is born without its instinctual patterns, there is no reason whatsoever to believe that man should be born without his specific forms of physiological and psychological reactions. As animals of the same kind show the same instinctual phenomena all over the world, man also shows the same archetypal forms no matter where he lives. As animals have no need to be taught their instinctive activities, so man also possesses his primordial psychic patterns and repeats them spontaneously, independently of any kind of teaching.

Inasmuch as man is conscious and capable of introspection, it is quite possible that he can perceive his instinctual patterns in the form of archetypal representations. As a matter of fact, these possess the expected degrees of universality, [as we see by] the remarkable identity of shamanistic structures. It is also possible to observe their spontaneous reproductions in individuals entirely ignorant of traditions of this sort. Such facts prove the autonomy of the arche-types. (3)

Just as in physics, we cannot observe nuclear processes directly, so there can be no direct observation of the contents of the collective unconscious. In both cases, their actual nature can be inferred only from their efforts, just as the trajectory of a nuclear particle in a Wilson cloud chamber can be traced only by observing the condensation trail that follows its movement and thus makes it visible.

In practice, we observe the archetype "traces" primarily in dreams, where they become perceptible as psychic forms. But this is not the only way they reach perception: they can appear objectively and concretely in the form of physical facts just as well. (3)

As soon as there are symptoms of a neurosis the diagnosis becomes uncertain, as one does not know prima vista whether you are confronted with the picture of the true character or of the opposite compensating character. Moreover, there are not a few introverts who are so painfully aware of the shortcomings of their attitude that they have learned to imitate the extraverts and behave accordingly, and vice versa, there are extraverts who like to give themselves the air of the introvert because they think they are then more interesting.

Although I have never made a statistic of this kind, I have always been impressed by the fact that pipe-smokers are usually introverted. The typical extravert is too much of a busybody to bother and fuss with the pipe, which demands infinitely more nursing than a cigarette that can be lighted or thrown away in a second.

That does not prevent me from having found heavy cigarette-smokers among my introverts and not a few pipe-smokers among the extraverts, but normally with empty pipes. Pipe smoking was in their case one of the cherished introverted mannerisms.

I cannot omit to remark that the diagnosis is not rarely hampered by the fact that it is chiefly extraverts who resent being called extraverts, as if it were a derogatory designation. I even know of a case where a famous extravert, having been called an extravert, challenged his opponent to a duel. (3)

The derogatory interpretations of the unconscious are usually due to the fact that the observer projects his primitivity and his blindness into the unconscious. He thereby pursues the secret goal of protecting himself against the inexorable demands of nature in the widest sense of the word.

As the term "unconscious" denotes, we don't know it. It is the unknown, of which we can say anything we like. Not one of our statements will be necessarily true. The reason why the unconscious appears to us in such a disagreeable form is because we are afraid of it, and we revile it because we hope that by this method we can free ourselves from its attractions. It is a puzzle—I admit—to anybody who occasionally indulges in thinking. (3)

A wrong functioning of the psyche can do much to injure the body. Just as conversely, a bodily illness can affect the psyche. For psyche and body are not separate entities, but one and the same life. (81)

The psyche consists essentially of images. It is a series of images in the truest sense: not an accidental juxtaposition or sequence, but a structure that is throughout full of meaning and purpose. It is a "picturing" of vital activities. And just as the material of the body that is ready for life has need of the psyche in order to be capable of life, so the psyche presupposes the living body in order that its images may live. (73)

Natural man is not a "self." He is the mass and a particle in the mass, collective to such a degree that he is not even sure of his own ego. That is why since time immemorial he has needed the transformation mysteries to turn him into something, and to rescue him from the animal collective psyche, which is nothing but an assortment, a "variety performance." (58)

It is not only primitive man whose psychology is archaic. It is the psychology also of modern, civilized man, and not merely of individual "throwbacks" in modern society. On the contrary, every civilized human being, however high his conscious development, is still an archaic man at the deepest levels of his psyche.

Just as the human body connects us with the mammals and displays numerous vestiges of earlier evolutionary stages going back even to the reptilian age, so the human psyche is a product of evolution which, when followed back to its origins, shows countless archaic traits. (18)

Just as a man has a body which is no different in principle from that of an animal, so also his psychology has a whole series of lower stories in which the specters from humanity's past epochs still dwell: the animal souls from the age of Pithecanthropus and the hominids, then the "psyche" of the cold-blooded saurians, and, deepest down of all, the transcendental mystery and paradox of the sympathetic and parasympathetic psychoid systems. (41)

Whatever name we may put to the psychic background, the fact remains that our consciousness is influenced by it in the highest degree, and all the more so the less we are conscious of it. The layman can hardly conceive how much his inclinations, moods, and decisions are influenced by the dark forces of his psyche, and how dangerous or helpful they may be in shaping his destiny.

Our cerebral consciousness is like an actor who has forgotten that he is playing a role. But when the play comes to an end, he must remember his own subjective reality, for he can no longer continue to live as Julius Caesar or as Othello, but only as himself, from whom he has become estranged by a momentary sleight of consciousness.

He must know once again that he was merely a figure on the stage who was playing a piece of Shakespeare, and that there was a director in the background who, as always, will have something very important to say about his acting. (96)

Empirical psychology loved, until recently, to explain the "unconscious" as mere absence of consciousness: the term itself indicates as much, just as shadow is an absence of light. Today accurate observation of unconscious processes has recognized, with all other ages before us, that the unconscious possesses a creative autonomy such as a mere shadow could never be endowed with. (60)

Since the stars have fallen from heaven and our highest symbols have paled, a secret life holds sway in the unconscious. That is why we have a psychology today, and why we speak of the unconscious. All this would be quite superfluous in an age or culture that possessed symbols.

Symbols are spirit from above, and under those conditions the spirit is above too. Therefore, it would be a foolish and senseless undertaking for such people to wish to experience or investigate an unconscious that contains nothing but the silent, undisturbed sway of nature.

Our unconscious [however] hides living water, spirit that has become nature, and that is why it is disturbed. Heaven has become for us the cosmic space of the physicists and the divine empyrean a fair memory of things that once were. But "the heart glows," and a secret unrest gnaws at the roots of our being. (19)

In the same way that the State has caught the individual, the individual imagines that he has caught the psyche and holds her in the hollow of his hand. He is even making a science of her in the absurd supposition that the intellect, which is but a part and a function of the psyche, is sufficient to comprehend the much greater whole.

In reality, the psyche is the mother and the maker, the subject and even the possibility of consciousness itself. It reaches so far beyond the boundaries of consciousness that the latter could easily be compared to an island in the ocean.

Whereas the island is small and narrow, the ocean is immensely wide and deep, and contains a life infinitely surpassing, in kind and degree, anything known on the island: so that if it is a question of space, it does not matter whether the gods are "inside" or "outside."

It might be objected that there is no proof that consciousness is nothing more than an island in the ocean. Certainly it is impossible to prove this, since the known range of consciousness is confronted with the unknown extension of the unconscious, of which we only know that it exists and by the very fact of its existence exerts a limiting effect on consciousness and its freedom. (60)

The dream is a little hidden doorway in the innermost and most secret recesses of the soul, opening into that cosmic night which was psyche long before there was any ego-consciousness, and which will remain psyche no matter how far our ego-consciousness extends.

For all ego-consciousness is isolated: because it separates and discriminates, it knows only particulars, and it sees only those that can be related to the ego. Its essence is limitation, even though it reaches to the farthest nebulae among the stars.

All consciousness separates; but in dreams we put on the likeness of that more universal, truer, more eternal man dwelling in the darkness of primordial night. There he is still the whole, and has whole in him, indistinguishable from nature and bare of all egohood. It is from these all-uniting depths that the dream arises, be it ever so childish, grotesque, and immoral. (6)

Dream psychology opens the way to a general comparative psychology from which we may hope to gain the same understanding of the development and structure of the human psyche as comparative anatomy has given us concerning the human body. (31)

A dream, like every element in the psychic structure, is a product of the total psyche. Hence we may expect to find in dreams everything that has ever been of significance in the life of humanity.

Just as human life is not limited to this or that fundamental instinct, but builds itself up from a multiplicity of instincts, needs, desires, and physical and psychic conditions, so the dream cannot be explained by this or that element in it, however beguilingly simple such an explanation may appear to be. We can be certain that it is incorrect, because no simple theory of instinct will ever be capable of grasping the human psyche, that mighty and mysterious thing; nor, consequently, its exponent, the dream. In order to do anything like justice to dreams, we need an interpretive equipment that must be laboriously fitted together from all branches of the humane sciences. (31)

Dreams are impartial, spontaneous products of the unconscious psyche, outside the control of the will. They are pure nature; they show us the unvarnished, natural truth, and are therefore fitted, as nothing else, to give us back an attitude that accords with our basic human nature when our consciousness has strayed too far from its foundations and run into an impasse. (96)

The dream shows the inner truth and reality of the patient as it really is: not as I conjecture it to be, and not as he would like it to be, but *as it is*. (50)

Dreams are as simple or as complicated as the dreamer is himself, only they are always a little bit ahead of the dreamer's consciousness. I do not understand my own dreams any better than any of you, for they are always somewhat beyond my grasp and I have the same trouble with them as anyone who knows nothing about dream interpretation. Knowledge is no advantage when it is a matter of one's own dreams. (4)

To confront a person with his own shadow is to show him his own light. Once one has experienced a few times what it is like to stand judgingly between the opposites, one begins to understand what is meant by the self. Anyone who perceives his shadow and his light simultaneously sees himself from two sides and thus gets in the middle. (33)

Everything that works from the unconscious appears projected on others. Not that these are wholly without blame, for even the worst projection is at least hung on a hook: perhaps a very small one, but still a hook offered by the other person. (45)

The intellect is only one among several fundamental psychic functions and therefore does not suffice to give a complete picture of the world. For this another function— feeling—is needed too. Feeling often arrives at convictions that are different from those of the intellect, and we cannot always prove the convictions of feeling are necessary. (55)

If science is an end itself, man's *raison d'être* lies in being a mere intellect. If art is an end itself, then his sole value lies in the imaginative faculty, and the intellect is consigned to the lumber-room. If making money is an end in itself, both science and art can quietly shut up shop. No one can deny that our modern consciousness, in pursuing these mutually exclusive ends, has become hopelessly fragmented. The consequence is that people are trained to develop one quality only: they become tools themselves. (16)

Consciousness is always only a part of the psyche and therefore never capable of psychic wholeness: for that the indefinite extension of the unconscious is needed. But the unconscious can neither be caught with clever formula nor exorcised by means of scientific dogmas, for something of destiny clings to it—indeed, it is sometimes destiny itself. (77)

Whoever looks into the mirror of the water will see first of all his own face. Whoever goes to himself risks a confrontation with himself. The mirror does not flatter, it faithfully shows whatever looks into it; namely, the face we never show to the world because we cover it with the *persona*, the mask of the actor. But the mirror lies behind the mask and shows the true face. (19)

Unfortunately, there can be no doubt that man is, on the whole, less good than he imagines himself or wants to be. Everyone carries a shadow, and the less it is embodied in the individual's conscious life, the blacker and denser it is. If an inferiority is conscious, one always has a chance to correct it. Furthermore, it is constantly in contact with interests, so that it is continually subjected to modifications. But if it is repressed and isolated from consciousness, it never gets corrected. (60)

If the repressed tendencies, the shadow as I call them, were obviously evil, there would be no problem whatever. But the shadow is merely somewhat inferior, primitive, unadapted, and awkward; not wholly bad. It even contains childish or primitive qualities which would, in a way, vitalize and embellish human existence, but—convention forbids. (60)

It would be a ridiculous and unwarranted assumption on our part if we imagined that we were more energetic or more intelligent than [those] of the past. Our material knowledge has increased, but not our intelligence. This means that we are just as bigoted in regard to new ideas, and just as impervious to them, as people were in the darkest days of antiquity. We have become rich in knowledge, but poor in wisdom. (78)

One would do well to treat every dream as though it were a totally unknown object. Look at it from all sides, take it in your hand, carry it about with you, let your imagination play round it, and talk about it with other people. Primitives tell each other impressive dreams, in a public palaver if posssible, and this custom is also attested in late antiquity, for all the ancient peoples attributed great significance to dreams.

Treated in this way, the dream suggests all manner of ideas and associations which lead us closer to its meaning. The ascertainment of the meaning is, I need hardly point out, an entirely arbitrary affair, and this is where the hazards begin.

Narrower or wider limits will be set to the meaning, according to one's experience, temperament, and taste. Some people will be satisfied with little, for others much is still not enough. Also, the meaning of the dream, or our interpretation of it, is largely dependent on the intentions of the interpreter, on what he expects the meaning to be or requires it to do. In eliciting the meaning, he will involuntarily be guided by certain presuppositions, and it depends very much on the scrupulousness and honesty of the investigator whether he gains something by his interpretation or perhaps only becomes still more deeply entangled in his mistakes. (96)

The real difficulty begins when the dreams do not point to anything tangible, and this they do often enough, especially when they hold anticipations of the future. I do not mean that such dreams are necessarily prophetic, merely that they feel the way, they "reconnoitre." These dreams contain inklings of possibilities and for that reason can never be made plausible to an outsider. (13)

Archetypes are like riverbeds which dry up when the water deserts them, but which it can find again at any time. An archetype is like an old watercourse along which the water of life has flowed for centuries, digging a deep channel for itself. The longer it has flowed in this channel, the more likely it is that sooner or later the water will return to its old bed. (87)

Our personal psychology is just a thin skin, a ripple on the ocean of collective psychology. The powerful factor—the factor which changes our whole life, which changes the surface of our known world, which makes history—is collective psychology, and [it] moves according to laws entirely different from those of our consciousness. The archetypes are the great decisive forces, they bring about the real events, and not our personal reasoning and practical intellect. . . . The archetypal images decide the fate of man. (4)

All the most powerful ideas in history go back to archetypes. This is particularly true of religious ideas, but the central concepts of science, philosophy, and ethics are no exception to this rule. In their present form, they are variants of archetypal ideas, created by consciously applying and adapting these ideas to reality. For it is the function of consciousness not only to recognize and assimilate the external world through the gateway of the senses, but to translate into visible reality the world within us. (76)

The great problems of life, including of course sex, are always related to the primordial images of the collective unconscious. These images are balancing and compensating factors that correspond to the problems which life confronts us with in reality. This is no matter for astonishment, since these images are deposits of thousands of years of experience of the struggle for existence and for adaptation.

Every great experience in life, every profound conflict, evokes the accumulated treasure of these images and brings about their inner constellation. But they become accessible to consciousness only when the individual possesses so much self-awareness and power of understanding that he also reflects on what he experiences instead of just living it blindly. In the latter event, he actually lives the myth and the symbol without knowing it. (56)

It is a very difficult and important question, what you call the technique of dealing with the shadow. There is, as a matter of fact, no technique at all, inasmuch as technique means that there is a known and perhaps even prescribable way to deal with a certain difficulty or task.

There is, for instance, no particular technique that would help us to reconcile two political parties opposing each other. It can be a question of good will, or diplomatic cunning or civil war, or anything. If one can speak of a technique at all, it consists solely in an attitude. First of all, one has to accept and to take seriously into account the existence of the shadow. Secondly, it is necessary to be informed about its qualities and intentions. Thirdly, long and difficult negotiations will be unavoidable. (3)

Our mind has its history, just as our body has its history. You might be just as astonished that man has an appendix, for instance. Does he know he ought to have an appendix? He is just born with it. Millions of people do not know they have a thymus, but they have it. They do not know that in certain parts of their anatomy they belong to the species of the fishes, and yet it is so.

Our unconscious mind, like our body, is a storehouse of relics and memories of the past. A study of the structure of the unconscious collective mind would reveal the same discoveries as you make in comparative anatomy. (4)

The deepest we can reach in our exploration of the unconscious mind is the layer where man is no longer a distinct individual, but where his mind widens out and merges into the mind of humanity—not the conscious mind, but the unconscious mind of humanity, where we are all the same.

As the body has its anatomical conformity in its two eyes and two ears and one heart and so on, with only slight individual differences, so has the mind its basic conformity. On this collective level, we are no longer separate individuals. We are all one. (4)

As a rule, when the collective unconscious becomes really constellated in larger social groups, the result is a public craze, a mental epidemic that may lead to revolution or war or something of the sort. These movements are exceedingly contagious—almost overwhelmingly contagious because, when the collective unconscious is activated, you are no longer the same person. You are not only in the movement—you are it. (4)

I do not like to analyze one dream alone, because a single dream can be interpreted arbitrarily. You can speculate anything about an isolated dream; but if you compare a series of, say, twenty or a hundred dreams, then you can see interesting things. You see the process that is going on in the unconscious psyche extending through day and night. Presumably we are dreaming all the time, although we are not aware of it by day because consciousness is much too clear. But at night . . . the dreams can break through and become visible. (4)

If a dream is clearly formed of *personal* material, you have to get to the individual associations; but if the dream is chiefly a *mythological* structure—a difference which is obvious at once—then it speaks a universal language, and you or I can supply parallels to construct the context as well as anybody else, always provided we possess the necessary knowledge.

For instance, when the dream takes up the hero-dragon conflict, everybody has something to say about it, because we have all read fairytales and legends and know something of heroes and dragons. On the collective level of dreams, there is practically no difference in human beings, while there is all the difference on the personal level. (4)

So these depths, that layer of utter unconsciousness in our dreams, contain at the same time the key to individual completeness and wholeness: in other words, to healing. The meaning of "whole" or "wholeness" is to make holy or to heal. The descent into the depths will bring healing. It is the way to the total being, to the treasure which suffering humanity is forever seeking, which is hidden in the place guarded by terrible danger. This is the place of primordial unconsciousness, and at the same time, the place of healing and redemption, because it contains the jewel of wholeness. (4)

Emotions are contagious because they are deeply rooted in the sympathetic system. Any process of an emotional kind immediately arouses similar processes in others. When you are in a crowd which is moved by an emotion, you cannot fail to be roused by that same emotion.

Suppose you are in a country where a language is spoken which you don't understand, and somebody makes a joke and people laugh, then you laugh too in an idiotic way, simply because you can't refrain from laughing. Also when you are in a crowd that is politically excited, you can't help being excited, too, even when you do not share their opinion at all, because emotion has this suggestive effect. (4)

All those personal things like incestuous tendencies and other childish tunes are mere surface; what the unconscious really contains are the great collective events of the time. In the collective unconscious of the individual, history prepares itself; and when the archetypes are activated in a number of individuals and come to the surface, we are in the midst of history. (4)

Just as our conscious thoughts often occupy themselves with the future and its possibilities, so do the unconscious and its dreams. There has long been a general belief that the chief function of dreams is prognostication of the future. In antiquity, and as late as the Middle Ages, dreams played their part in medical prognosis. (5)

The collective unconscious—so far as we can say anything about it at all—appears to consist of mythological motifs or primordial images, for which reason the myths of all nations are its real exponents. In fact, the whole of mythology could be taken as a sort of projection of the collective unconscious. (76)

The deposit of humanity's whole ancestral existence—so rich in emotional imagery—of father, mother, child, husband and wife, of the magic personality, of dangers to body and soul, has exalted this group of archetypes into the supreme regulating principles of religious and even political life, in unconscious recognition of their tremendous psychic power. (76)

The collective unconscious contains the whole spiritual heritage of humanity's evolution, born anew in the brain structure of every individual. His conscious mind is an ephemeral phenomenon that accomplishes all provisional adaptations and orientations, for which reason one can best compare its function to orientation in space.

The unconscious, [however], is the source of the instinctual forces of the psyche and of the forms or categories that regulate them: namely, the archetypes. All the most powerful ideas in history go back to archetypes. This is particularly true of religious ideas, but the concepts of science, philosophy, and ethics are no exception to this rule. In their present form, they are variants of archetypal ideas, created by consciously applying and adapting these ideas to reality. For it is the function of consciousness not only to recognize and assimilate the external world through the gateway of the senses, but to translate into visible reality the world within us. (76)

The unconscious, as the totality of all archetypes, is the deposit of all human experience right back to its remotest beginnings. Not, indeed, a dead deposit, a sort of abandoned rubbish-heap, but a living system of reactions and aptitudes that determine the individual's life in invisible ways—all the more effective because invisible. It is not just a gigantic, historical prejudice, so to speak, an *a priori* historical condition; it is also the source of the instinct, for the archetypes are simply the forms which the instincts assume.

From the living fountain of instinct flows everything that is creative; hence, the unconscious is not merely conditioned by history, but is the very source of the creative impulse. (76)

While the personal unconscious is made up essentially of contents which have at one time been conscious but which have disappeared from consciousness through having been forgotten or repressed, the contents of the collective unconscious have never been in consciousness, and therefore have never been individually acquired, but owe their existence exclusively to heredity. Whereas the personal unconscious consists for the most part of complexes, the content of the collective unconscious is made up essentially of archetypes. (97)

By "active imagination," I mean a sequence of fantasies produced by deliberate concentration. I have found that the existence of unrealized, unconscious fantasies increases the frequency and intensity of dreams, and that when these fantasies are made conscious, the dreams change their character and become weaker and less frequent. From this, I have drawn the conclusion that dreams often contain fantasies which "want" to become conscious. (97)

A very common instance [of psychic *inflation*] is the humorless way in which many men identify themselves with their business or their titles. . . . When, therefore, I identify myself with my office or title, I behave as though I myself were the whole complex of social factors of which that office consists, or as though I were not only the bearer of the office, but also and at the same time the approval of society. I have made an extraordinary extension of myself, and have usurped qualities which are not in me but outside me. (89)

Since human nature is not compounded wholly of light, but also abounds in shadows, the insight gained in practical analysis is often somewhat painful, the more so if, as is generally the case, one has previously neglected the other side. Hence, there are people who take their newly won insight very much to heart—far too much, in fact, forgetting that they are not unique in having a shadow-side. They allow themselves to get unduly depressed, and are then inclined to doubt everything, finding nothing right anywhere. (89)

Identification with one's office or title is very attractive indeed, which is precisely why so many [people] are nothing more than the decorum accorded to them by society. In vain, one would look for a personality behind the mask. Underneath all the padding, one would find a very pitiable little creature. That is why the office—or whatever this outer husk may be—is so attractive: it offers easy compensation for personal deficiencies. (89)

Just as one [person] may disappear in his social role, so another may be engulfed by his inner vision and be lost to his surroundings. Many fathomless transformations of personality, like sudden conversions and other far-reaching changes of mind, originate in the attractive power of a collective image. (89)

The specific virtues and vices of humanity are contained in the collective psyche like everything else. (89)

To find out what is truly individual in ourselves, profound reflection is needed: and suddenly we realize how uncommonly difficult the discovery of individuality is.

A sign is always less than the thing it points to, and a symbol is always more than we can understand at first sight. Therefore, we never stop at the sign but go on to the goal it indicates; but we remain with the symbol because it promises more than it reveals. (5)

Fundamentally, the *persona* is nothing real: it is a compromise between individual and society as to what a man should appear to be. He takes a name, earns a title, exercises a function, he is this or that. In a certain sense, all this is real. Yet, in relation to the essential individuality of the person concerned it is only a secondary reality. (89)

Lack of conscious understanding does not mean that the dream has no effect at all. Even civilized man can occasionally observe that a dream which he cannot remember can slightly alter his mood for better or worse. Dreams can be "understood" to a certain extent in a subliminal way, and that is mostly how they work. (5)

How is one to know whether his dream is a "big" or a "little" one? He knows it by an instinctive feeling of significance. He feels so overwhelmed by the impression it makes that he would never think of keeping the dream to himself. He *has* to tell it, on the psychologically correct assumption that it is of general importance. (89)

Rational truths are not the last word, there are also irrational ones. In human affairs, what appears impossible by way of the intellect has often become true by way of the irrational. Indeed, all the greatest changes that have ever affected humanity have come not by way of intellectual calculation, but by ways which contemporary minds either ignored or rejected as absurd, and which were recognized only long afterward because of their intrinsic necessity. More often than not, they are never recognized at all, for the all-important laws of mental development are still a book with seven seals. (56)

Everything old in our unconscious hints at something coming. (56)

# CHILDHOOD, CHILDREN, AND PARENTING

Our consciousness does not create itself. It wells up from unknown depths. In childhood it awakens gradually, and all through life it wakes each morning out of the depths of sleep from an unconscious condition. (61)

Though a child is not born conscious, his mind is not a *tabula rasa*. The child is born with a definite brain . . . with a finished structure, but this brain has its history. It has been built up in the course of millions of years and represents a history of which it is the result. Naturally, it carries with it the traces of that history, exactly like the body, and if you grope down into the basic structure of the mind, you naturally find traces of the archaic mind. (4)

In early childhood, a character is already there. A child is not born as a *tabula rasa* as one assumes. The child is born as a high complexity, with existing determinants that never waver through the whole life, and that gives the child his character. Already, in earliest childhood, a mother recognizes the individuality of her child; and so, if you observe carefully, you see a tremendous difference, even in small children.

These peculiarities express themselves in every way. First . . . in all childish activities: in the way [the child] plays, in the things it is interested in.

There are children who are tremendously interested in moving things, in the movement chiefly, and in all things they see that affect the body. So they are interested in what the eyes do, what the ears do, how far you can bore into the nose with your finger . . .

These interests express themselves in a typically childish way in children. Later on, they express themselves in other peculiarities which are still the same, but it doesn't come from the fact that they once had done such and such a thing in childhood. It is the character that is doing it. There is a definite inherited complexity. (1)

If there is anything that we wish to change in our children, we should first examine it and see whether it is not something that could better be changed in ourselves.

Take our enthusiasm for pedagogics. It may be that the boot is on the other leg. It may be that we misplace the pedagogical need because it would be an uncomfortable reminder that we ourselves are still children in many respects and still need a vast amount of educating. (26)

Our whole educational problem suffers from a one-sided approach to the child who is to be educated, and from an equally one-sided lack of emphasis on the un-educatedness of the educator. (26)

One looks back with appreciation to the brilliant teachers, but with gratitude to those who touched our human feelings. The curriculum is so much necessary raw material, but warmth is the vital element for the growing plant and for the soul of the child. (32)

A child certainly allows himself to be impressed by the grand talk of his parents, but do they really imagine he is educated by it? Actually, it is the parents' lives that educate the child: what they add by word and gesture at best serves only to confuse him. The same holds good for the teacher. But we have such a belief in method that, if only the method be good, the practice of it seems to sanctify the teacher. (56)

No doubt we are right to open the eyes and ears of our young people to the wide world, but it is the maddest of delusions to think that this really equips them for the task of living. It is the kind of training that enables a young person to adapt himself outwardly to the world and reality, but no one gives a thought to the necessity of adapting to the self, to the powers of the psyche, which are far mightier than all the Great Powers of the earth. (40)

Nothing exerts a stronger psychic effect upon the human environment, and especially upon children, than the life which the parents have not lived. (47)

All the life which the parents could have lived, but of which they thwarted themselves for artificial motives, is passed on to the children in substitute form. That is to say, the children are driven unconsciously in a direction that is intended to compensate for everything that was left unfulfilled in the lives of their parents. Hence, it is that excessively moral-minded parents have what are called "unmoral children," or an irresponsible wastrel of a father has a son with a positively morbid amount of ambition, and so on. (39)

To remain a child too long is childish, but it is just as childish to move away and then assume that childhood no longer exists because we do not see it. But if we return to the "children's land" we succumb to the fear of becoming childish, because we do not understand that everything of psychic origin has a double face. One face looks forward, the other back. It is ambivalent and therefore symbolic, like all living reality. (58)

Childhood is important not only because various warpings of instinct have their origin there, but because this is the time when, terrifying or encouraging, those far-seeing dreams and images appear before the soul of the child, shaping his whole destiny, as well as those retrospective intuitions which reach back far beyond the range of childhood experiences into the life of our ancestors. Thus in the child-psyche the natural condition is already opposed by a "spiritual" one. (45)

Fairytales seem to be the myths of childhood and they therefore contain among other things the mythology which children weave for themselves concerning sexual processes. The poetry of fairytale, whose magic is felt even by the adult, rests not least upon the fact that some of the old theories are still alive in our unconscious. We experience a strange and mysterious feeling whenever a fragment of our remotest youth stirs into life again, not actually reaching consciousness, but merely shedding a reflection of its emotional intensity on the conscious mind. (52)

If we try to extract the common and essential factors from the almost inexhaustible variety of individual problems found in the period of youth, we meet in all cases with one particular feature: a more-or-less patent clinging to the childhood level of consciousness, a resistance to the fateful forces in and around us which would involve us in the world. . . .

In all this, there is something of the inertia of matter. It is a persistence in the previous state whose range of consciousness is smaller, narrower, and more egoistic than of the dualistic phase. For here the individual is faced with the necessity of recognizing and accepting what is different and strange as part of his own life. (74)

We know that the first impressions of childhood accompany us inalienably throughout life, and that, just as indestructibly, certain educational influences can keep people all their lives within those limits. In these circumstances, it is not surprising that conflicts break out between the personality molded by educational and other influences of the infantile milieu and one's own individual style of life. It is a conflict which all those must face who are called upon to live a life that is independent and creative. (79)

It is, of course, impossible to free oneself from one's childhood without devoting a great deal of work to it, as Freud's researches have long since shown. Nor can it be achieved through intellectual knowledge alone; what is alone effective is a remembering that is also a re-experiencing. The swift passage of years and the overwhelming inrush of the newly discovered world leave a mass of material behind that is never dealt with. We do not shake this off; we merely remove ourselves from it. So that when, in later years, we return to the memories of childhood, we find bits of our personality still alive, which cling round us and suffuse us with the feeling of earlier times. Being still in their childhood state, these fragments are very powerful in their effect. (95)

In every adult there lurks a child—an eternal child, something that is always becoming, is never completed, and calls for unceasing care, attention, and education. That is the part of the human personality which wants to develop and become whole. But the man of today is far indeed from this wholeness. (26)

Something in us wishes to remain a child, to be unconscious or, at most, conscious only of the ego: to reject everything strange, or else subject it to our will. In all this, there is something of the inertia of matter. (74)

In principle, I am always in favor of children leaving their parents as soon as possible once they have reached maturity. Parents must realize that they are trees from which the fruit falls in the autumn. Children don't belong to their parents, and they are only apparently produced by them.

In reality, they come from a thousand-year-old stem, or rather from many stems, and often they are about as characteristic of their parents as an apple from a fir-tree. Beyond the human obligation to look after aging parents and to maintain a friendly relation with them, there should be no other dependents, for the younger generation has to start life anew and can encumber itself with the past only in case of the greatest necessity. (3)

The high ideal of educating the personality is not for children: for what is usually meant by personality, a well-rounded psychic whole that is capable of resistance and abounding in energy—is an *adult ideal.* It is only in an age like ours, when the individual is unconscious of the problems of adult life, or—what is worse—when he consciously shirks from them, that people could wish to foist this ideal onto childhood. (26)

What we call [personality] development or progress is going round and round a central point in order to get gradually closer to it. In reality, we always remain on the same spot, just a little nearer to or further from the center. Even as a child, I had alchemical insights which would sound much more astonishing than anything I said about them in my libido book. Other people have them too. Originally we were all born out of a world of wholeness, and in the first years of life, are still completely contained in it. Later we lose it, and call it progress when we remember it again. (3)

# INDIVIDUATION: BECOMING YOUR TRUE SELF

Everything living dreams of individuation, for everything strives towards its own wholeness. (3)

It is part of the business of growing up to listen to the fearful discords which real life grinds out and to include them among the images of reality. Truth and reality are assuredly no music of the spheres—they are the beauty and terror of Nature herself. (23)

For indeed our consciousness does not create itself—it wells up from unknown depths. In childhood it awakens gradually, and all through life it wakes each morning out of the depths of sleep from an unconscious condition. It is like a child that is born daily out of the primordial womb of the unconscious. (6)

Our personality develops in the course of our life from germs that are hard or impossible to discern, and it is only our deeds that reveal who we are. (26)

It is not possible to live too long amid the infantile surroundings, or in the bosom of the family, without endangering one's psychic health. Life calls us forth to independence, and anyone who does not heed this call because of childish laziness or timidity is threatened with neurosis.

And once this has broken out, it becomes an increasingly valid reason for running away from life and remaining forever in the morally poisonous atmosphere of infancy. (78)

The hero's main feat is to overcome the monster of darkness; it is only the long-hoped-for and expected triumph of consciousness over the unconscious. The coming of consciousness was probably the most tremendous experience of primeval times, for with it a world came into being whose existence no one had suspected before. "And God said, `Let there be light' " is the projection of that immemorial experience of the separation of consciousness from the unconscious. (62)

Man started from an unconscious state and has ever striven for greater consciousness. The development of consciousness is the burden, the suffering, and the blessing of mankind. (8)

"But why on earth?" you may ask, "should it be necessary for man to achieve, by hook or crook, a higher level of consciousness?" This is truly the crucial question, and I do not find the answer easy. Instead of a real answer, I can only make a confession of faith: I believe that, after thousands and millions of years, someone had to realize that this wonderful world of mountains and oceans, suns and moons, galaxies and nebulae, plants and animals, *exists.*

From a low hill in the Athi plains of East Africa, I once watched the vast herds of wild animals grazing in soundless stillness, as they had done from time immemorial, touched only by the breath of a primeval world. I felt then as if I were the first man, the first creature, to know that all this *is.*

The entire world round me was still in its primeval state;

it did not know that it *was*. And then, in that one moment in which I came to know, the world sprang into being; without that moment, it never would have been. All Nature seeks this goal and finds it fulfilled in man, but only in the most highly developed and most fully conscious man. (54)

If you do not go along with the unconscious properly, that is, if it finds no expression through consciousness and conscious action, it piles up libido in the body and this leads to physical [weaknesses]. (3)

The aim of individuation is nothing less than to divest the self of the false wrappings of the persona on the one hand, and of the suggestive power of primordial images on the other. (89)

Nothing is so apt to challenge our self-awareness and alertness as being at war with oneself. One can hardly think of any other or more effective means of waking humanity out of the irresponsible and innocent half-sleep of the primitive mentality and bringing it to a state of conscious responsibility. (57)

The very frequent neurotic disturbances of adult years all have one thing in common: they want to carry the psychology of the youthful phase over the threshold of the so-called years of discretion. Who does not know those touching old gentlemen who must always warm up the dish of their student days, who can fan the flame of life only by reminiscences of their heroic youth, but who, for the rest, are stuck in a hopelessly wooden Philistinism?

As a rule, to be sure, they have this one merit which it

would be wrong to undervalue; they are not neurotic, but only boring and stereotyped. The neurotic is rather a person who can never have things as he would like them in the present, and who can therefore never enjoy the past either. (74)

Wholly unprepared, we embark upon the second half of life. Or are there perhaps colleges for forty-year-olds which prepare them for their coming life and its demands as the ordinary colleges introduce our young people to a knowledge of the world? No, thoroughly unprepared we take the step into the afternoon of life; worse still, we take this step with the false assumption that our truths and ideals will serve as hitherto. But we cannot live the afternoon of life according to the program of life's morning; for what was great in the morning will be little at evening, and what was [true] in the morning will at evening have become a lie. (74)

The middle period of life is a time of enormous psychological importance. The child begins its psychological life within very narrow limits, inside the magic circle of the mother and the family. With progressive maturation it widens its horizon and its own sphere of influence; its hopes and intentions are directed to extending the scope of personal power and possessions; desire reaches out to the world in ever-widening range; the will of the individual becomes more and more identical with the natural goals pursued by unconscious motivations.

Thus man breathes his own life into things, and finally they begin to live of themselves and to multiply; and imperceptibly he is overgrown by them. Mothers are overtaken by their children, men by their own creations, and what was originally brought into being only with labor and the greatest effort can no longer be held in check. First it was passion, then it became duty, and finally an intolerable burden, a vampire that battens on the life of its creator. (39)

The greater the tension, the greater is the potential. Great energy springs from a correspondingly great tension between opposites. (48)

It is of the greatest importance for the young person, who is still unadapted and has as yet achieved nothing, to shape his conscious ego as effectively as possible, that is, to educate his will. Unless he is a positive genius he cannot, indeed he should not, believe in anything active within him that is not identical with his will. He must feel himself a man of will, and may safely depreciate everything else in him and deem it subject to his will, for without this illusion he could not succeed in adapting himself socially.

It is otherwise with a person in the second half of life who no longer needs to educate his conscious will, but who, to understand the meaning of his individual life, needs to experience his own inner being. Social usefulness is no longer an aim for him, although he does not deny its desirability. Fully aware as he is of the social unimportance of his creative activity, he feels it more as a way of working at himself to his own benefit. Increasingly, too, this activity frees him from morbid dependence, and he thus acquires an inner stability and a new trust in himself. (13)

An individual is infantile because he has freed himself insufficiently, or not at all, from his childish environment and his adaptation to his parents, with the result that he has a false reaction to the world; on the one hand, he reacts as a child toward his parents, always demanding love and immediate emotional rewards, while on the other hand, he is so identified with his parents through his close ties with them that he behaves like his father or his mother. He is incapable of living his own life and finding the character that belongs to him. (78)

Formerly, men called the gods unfavorable [during a person's difficulties]; now we prefer to call it a neurosis, and seek the cause in lack of vitamins, in endocrine disturbances, overwork, or sex. The cooperation of the unconscious, which is something we never think of and always take for granted is, when it suddenly fails, a very serious matter indeed. (28)

Individuation is not "individualization," but a conscious realization of everything the existence of an individual implies: his needs, his tasks, his duties, his responsibilities. Individuation does not isolate, it connects. I never saw relationships thriving on unconsciousness. (3)

The essential thing is to differentiate oneself from these unconscious contents by personifying them, and at the same time to bring them into relationship with consciousness. That is the technique for stripping them of their power. It is not too difficult to personify them, as they always possess a certain degree of autonomy, a separate identity of their own. Their autonomy is a most uncomfortable thing to reconcile oneself to, and yet the very fact that the unconscious presents itself in that way gives us the best means of handling it. (6)

The individual who wishes to have an answer to the problem of evil, as it is posed today, has need, first and fore-

most, of self-knowledge: that is, the utmost possible knowledge of his own wholeness. He must know relentlessly how
much good he can do, and what crimes he is capable of, and
must beware of regarding the one as real and the other as illusion. Both are elements within his nature, and both are
bound to come to light in him, should he wish—as he
ought—to live without deception or self-delusion.

In general, though, most people are hopelessly ill-
equipped for living on this level, although there are also
many persons who have the capacity for profounder insight into themselves. Such self-knowledge is of prime importance, because through it we approach that fundamental
stratum or core of human nature where the instincts dwell.
Here are those pre-existent dynamic factors concerning
which we cannot pass any final judgment. Our ideas about
it are bound to be inadequate, for we are unable to comprehend its essence cognitively and set rational limits to it.

We achieve knowledge of nature only through science, which enlarges consciousness; hence deepened self-
knowledge also requires science, that is, psychology. No one
builds a telescope or microscope with one turn of the wrist,
out of good will alone, without a knowledge of optics. (6)

Individuation means becoming a single, homogenous
being, and, in so far as "individuality" embraces our innermost, last, and incomparable uniqueness, it also implies
becoming one's own self. We could therefore translate individuation as "coming to selfhood" or "self-realization." (6)

What is sublimation? The term has been taken from
alchemy. . . . It means that you don't do what you really
wish to do, and play the piano instead. That is nice, you see!
Or, instead of giving way to your terrible passions, you go
to Sunday school. Then you say you have sublimated it—
"it!" It is, of course, an act of volition.

Even sublimation, which is a very useful and heroic thing, sometimes looks a bit funny. But it's never a serious thing, and it is certainly a way of dealing with the difficulties of life, all those difficulties that are forced upon us by our original nature.

We have a very unruly and passionate nature, perhaps, and we simply hurt ourselves if we live it in an uncontrolled way. Try to tell the truth. You would like to tell the truth, I am sure. Nobody likes to lie if he is not forced to. But just tell the truth for twenty-four hours and see what happens! In the end you can't stand yourself anymore.

So, you see, you can't let go of all your ambitions; you can't express your admiration to every pretty woman you see. You must control yourself, after all, and that is also a considerable piece of sublimation.

Take swearing: you must not use this impossible language, and so, instead of saying something disagreeable, you say something agreeable, as you have learnt, and all that continues—ethics, self-repression, and sublimation. And the worse your passions are, the more you must use this sublimation mechanism; otherwise you get into hot water. And you don't like that, either. (2)

Since the sole carrier of life and the quintessence of any kind of community is the individual, it follows that he and his quality are of paramount importance. The individual must be complete and have substance, otherwise nothing has substance—for any number of zeros still do not amount to more than zero.

A group of inferior people is never better than any one of them. It is just as inferior as they, and a State composed of nothing but sheep is never anything else but a herd of sheep, even though it is led by a shepherd with a vicious dog. (3)

When a hundred intelligent heads are united in a group, the result usually is one big fathead. (3)

I give the adaptation of the individual to society its full due. But I will still stand up for the inalienable rights of the individual, since he alone is the carrier of life and is gravely threatened by the social leveling process today. Even in the smallest group, he is accepted only if he appears acceptable to the majority of its members. He has to resign himself to being tolerated.

But mere toleration is no improvement: on the contrary, it fosters self-doubt, to which the isolated individual who has something to espouse is particularly prone. I am no preacher of "splendid isolation" and have the greatest difficulty in shielding myself from the crushing demands of people and human relationships. Without values of one's own, even social relationships lack significance. (3)

The sense of security is increased and the sense of responsibility is decreased when one is part of a group. Once I ran into a thick fog while crossing a treacherous glacier, full of crevasses, with a company of soldiers. The situation was so dangerous that everyone had to stop just where he happened to be. Yet there was no trace of panic, but rather the spirit of a public festival!

Had one been alone, or had there been two of us, the danger could not have been overlooked or laughed off. As it was, the brave and experienced had a chance to shine. The timid took heart from the plucky ones, and nobody said a word about the possibility of having to improvise a bivouac on the glacier, which could hardly have passed off without frostbite [and other problems], let alone about the perils of an attempted descent. This is typical of the mass mentality. (3)

The acorn can become an oak, and not a donkey. Nature will take its course. A man or woman becomes that which he or she is from the beginning. (1)

There are many people who are only partially conscious. Even among absolutely civilized [people] there is a disproportionally high number of abnormally unconscious individuals who spend a great part of their lives in an unconscious state. They know what happens to them, but they do not know what they do or say. They cannot judge of the consequences of their actions.

These are people who are abnormally unconscious: that is, in a primitive state. What then finally makes them conscious? If they get a slap in the face, then they become conscious: something really happens, and that makes them conscious. They meet with something fatal and then they suddenly realize what they are doing. (20)

People will do anything, no matter how absurd, in order to avoid facing their own souls. They will practice Indian yoga and all its exercises, observe a strict regimen of diet, learn the literature of the whole world—all because they cannot get on with themselves and have not the slightest faith that anything useful could ever come out of their own souls.

Thus the soul has gradually been turned into a Nazareth from which nothing good can come. Therefore, let us fetch it from the four corners of the earth: the more far-fetched and bizarre it is the better! (58)

Every advance in culture is, psychologically, an extension of consciousness, a coming to consciousness that can take place only through individuation. Therefore, an advance always begins with individuation: that is to say, with the individual, conscious of his isolation, cutting a new path through hitherto untrodden territory.

To do this, he must first return to the fundamental facts of his own being, irrespective of all authority and tradition, and allow himself to become conscious of his distinctiveness. If he succeeds in giving collective validity to his widened consciousness, he creates a tension of opposites that provides the stimulation which culture needs for its further progress. (45)

Achievement and usefulness are the ideals that seem to point the way out of the confusions of the problematical state. They are the lodestars that guide us in the adventure of broadening and consolidating our physical existence. They help us to strike our roots in the world, but they cannot guide us in the development of that wider consciousness to which we give the name of culture. In the period of youth, however, this course is the normal one, and in all circumstances preferable to merely tossing about in a welter of problems. (74)

Being old is highly unpopular. Nobody seems to consider that not being able to grow old is just as absurd as not being able to outgrow child's-size shoes. A still infantile man of thirty is surely to be deplored, but a youthful septuagenarian—isn't that delightful?

And yet, both are perverse, lacking in style—psychological monstrosities. A young man who does not fight and conquer has missed the best part of his youth, and an old man who does not know how to listen to the secrets of the brooks, as they tumble down from the peaks to the valleys, makes no sense: he is a spiritual mummy who is nothing but a rigid relic of the past. He stands apart from life, mechanically repeating himself to the last triviality! (72)

In the case of psychological suffering, which always isolates the individual from the herd of so-called normal people, it is of the greatest importance to understand that the conflict is not a personal failure only, but at the same time, a suffering common to all and a problem with which the whole epoch is burdened. This general viewpoint lifts the individual out of himself and connects him with humanity. (4)

Human beings have one faculty which, though it is of the greatest utility for collective purposes, is most pernicious for individuation, and that is the faculty of imitation. Collective psychology cannot dispense with imitation, for without it all mass organizations, the State and the social order, are impossible.

Society is organized, indeed, less by law than the propensity to imitation, implying equally suggestibility, suggestion, and mental contagion. But we see every day how people use, or rather abuse, the mechanism of imitation for the purpose of personal differentiation: they are content to ape some eminent personality, some striking characteristic or mode of behavior, thereby achieving an outward distinction from the circle in which they move.

We could almost say that as a punishment for this the uniformity of their minds with those of their neighbors, already real enough, is intensified into an unconscious, compulsive bondage to the environment. As a rule, these specious attempts at individual differentiation stiffen into a pose, and the imitator remains at the same level as he always was, only several degrees more sterile than before.

To find out what is truly individual in ourselves, profound reflection is needed; and suddenly we realize how uncommonly difficult the discovery of individuality is. (89)

The element of differentiation is the individual. All the highest achievements of virtue, as well as the blackest villainies, are individual. The larger a community is, and the more the sum total of collective factors peculiar to every large community rests on conservative prejudices detrimental to individuality, the more will the individual be morally and spiritually crushed, and, as a result, the one source of moral and spiritual progress for society is choked up.

Naturally, the only thing that can thrive in such an atmosphere is sociality and whatever is collective in the individual. Everything individual in him goes under: that is, is doomed to repression. The individual elements lapse into the unconscious, where, by the law of necessity, they are transformed into something essentially baleful, destructive, and anarchical.

Socially, this evil principle shows itself in the spectacular crimes—regicide and the like—perpetrated by certain prophetically-inclined individuals. But in the great mass of the community, it remains in the background, and only manifests itself indirectly in the inexorable moral degeneration of society. (89)

We do not sufficiently distinguish between individualism and individuation. Individualism means deliberately stressing and giving prominence to some supposed peculiarity, rather than to collective considerations and obligations. But individuation means precisely the better and more complete fulfillment of the collective qualities of the human being, since adequate consideration of the peculiarity of the individual is more conducive to better social achievement than when the peculiarity is neglected or suppressed. (89)

❖    ❖    ❖

No doubt it is a great nuisance that humanity is not uniform, but compounded of individuals whose psychic structure spreads them over a span of at least ten thousand years. Hence, there is absolutely no truth that does not spell salvation for one person and damnation to another. All universalisms get stuck in this terrible dilemma. (58)

Whenever an inferiority complex exists, there is good reason for it. There actually is an inferiority somewhere, though not just where one supposes it is. Modesty and humility are not signs of an inferiority complex. They are highly estimable, indeed admirable virtues and not complexes. They prove that their fortunate possessor is not a presumptuous fool but knows his limitations, and will therefore never stumble beyond the bounds of humanity, dazzled and intoxicated by his imagined greatness. (25)

One can fall victim to possession if one does not understand betimes why one is possessed. One should ask oneself for once: Why has this idea taken possession of me? What does that mean in regard to myself? A modest doubt like this can save us from falling head first into the idea and vanishing forever. (35)

The ego-conscious personality is only a part of the whole man, and its life does not yet represent his total life. The more he is merely "I," the more he splits himself off from the collective man, of whom he is also a part, and may even find himself in opposition to him.

But since everything living strives for wholeness, the inevitable one-sidedness of our conscious life is continually being corrected and compensated by the universal human being in us, whose goal is the ultimate integration of conscious and unconscious, or better, the assimilation of the ego to a wider personality. (43)

Complete human beings are exceptions. It is true that an overwhelming majority of educated people are fragmentary personalities and have a lot of substitutes instead of the genuine goods. (60)

Personality is a seed that can only develop by slow stages throughout life. There is no personality without definiteness, wholeness, and ripeness. These three qualities cannot and should not be expected of the child, as they would rob it of childhood. (26)

Personality can never develop unless the individual chooses his own way, consciously and with moral deliberation. Not only the causal motive—necessity—but conscious moral decision must lend its strength to the process of building the personality. If the first is lacking, then the alleged development is a mere act of will; if the second, it will get stuck in unconscious automatism. But a man can make a moral decision to go his own way only if he holds that way to be the best. If any other way were held to be better, then he would live and develop that other personality instead of his own.

The other ways are conventionalities of a moral, social, political, philosophical, or religious nature. The fact that the conventions always flourish in one form or another only proves that the vast majority of humanity do not choose their own way, but convention, and consequently develop not themselves but a method and a collective mode of life at the cost of their wholeness. (26)

Personality consists of two things: first, consciousness and whatever this covers, and second, an indefinitely large hinterland of unconscious psyche. So far as the former is concerned, it can be more-or-less clearly defined and delimited; but as for the sum total of human personality, one has to admit the impossibility of a complete description or definition.

In other words, there is bound to be an illimitable and indefinable addition to every personality, because the latter consists of a conscious and observable part which does not contain certain factors whose existence, however, we are forced to assume in order to explain observable facts. The unknown factors form what we call the unconscious part of the personality. (60)

The difference between the "natural" individuation process, which runs its course unconsciously, and the one which is consciously realized, is tremendous. In the first case, consciousness nowhere intervenes; the end remains as dark as the beginning. In the second case, so much darkness comes to light that the personality is permeated with light, and consciousness necessarily gains in scope and insight. The encounter between conscious and unconscious has to ensure that the light which shines in the darkness is not only comprehended by the darkness, but comprehends it. (17)

We cannot rate reason highly enough, but there are times when we must ask ourselves: do we really know enough about the destinies of individuals to entitle us to give good advice under *all* circumstances? Certainly, we must act according to our best convictions, but are we so sure that our convictions are for the best as regards the other person? Very often we do not know what is best for ourselves, and in later years, we may occasionally thank God from the bottom of our hearts that his kindly hand has preserved us from the "reasonableness" of our former plans.

It is easy for the critic to say after the event, "Ah, but then it wasn't the right sort of reason!" Who can know with unassailable certainty when he has the right sort? Moreover, is it not essential to the true art of living, sometimes, in defiance of all reason and fitness, to include the unreasonable and the unfitting within the ambiance of the possible? (63)

It is the task of the conscious mind to understand these hints. If this does not happen, the process of individuation will nevertheless continue. The only difference is that we become its victims and are dragged along by fate toward the inescapable goal which we might have reached walking upright, if only we had taken the trouble and been patient enough to understand the meaning of the numina that cross our path. (17)

Sure, if society consisted of valuable individuals only, adaptation would be worthwhile; but in reality, it is composed mainly of nincompoops and moral weaklings, and its level is far below that of its better representatives, in addition to which the mass as such stifles all individual values. . . . Conspicuous virtues are relatively rare and are mostly individual achievements. Mental and moral sloth, cowardice, bigotry, and unconsciousness dominate everything. (3)

A person who is unconscious of himself acts in a blind, instinctive way, and, is, in addition, fooled by all the illusions that arise when he sees everything that he is not conscious of in himself coming to meet him from outside as projections upon his neighbor. (49)

When one unconsciously works against oneself, the result is impatience, irritability, and an impotent longing to get one's opponent down whatever the means. Generally certain symptoms appear, among them a peculiar use of language: one wants to speak forcefully in order to impress one's opponent, so one employs a special "bombastic" style full of neologisms which might be described as "power-words."

This symptom is observable not only in the psychiatric clinic, but also among certain modern philosophers, and above all, whenever anything unworthy of belief has to be insisted on in the teeth of inner resistance: the language swells up, overreaches itself, sprouts grotesque words distinguished only by their needless complexity. The word is charged with the task of achieving what cannot be done by honest means. It is the old word magic, and sometimes it can degenerate into a regular disease. (48)

Everyone who becomes conscious of even a fraction of his unconscious gets outside his own time and social stratum into a kind of solitude. (3)

There are people who by nature are loving and kind, just as there are people who by nature believe and trust. For them love and faith are natural expressions of life which also benefit their fellow men. For the others, less gifted or not gifted at all, these are barely attainable ideals, a convulsive effort which is felt by their fellows too. (3)

Individuation does not shut one out from the world, but gathers the world to oneself. (44)

# THE PERSONAL IS ALSO GLOBAL

The psychology of the individual can never be exhaustively explained from himself alone: a clear recognition is needed by the way it is also conditioned by historical and environmental circumstances. His individual psychology is not merely a physiological, biological, or personal problem; it is also a contemporary problem. (56)

No one can claim to be immune to the spirit of his own epoch to possess anything like a complete knowledge of it. Regardless of our conscious convictions, we are all without exception, in so far as we are particles in the mass, gnawed at and undermined by the spirit that runs through the masses. Our freedom extends only so far as our consciousness reaches. (48)

Incisive changes in history are generally attributed exclusively to external causes. It seems to me, however, that external circumstances often serve merely as occasions for a new attitude to life and the world, long prepared in the unconscious, to become manifest. Social, political, and religious conditions affect the collective unconscious in the sense that all those factors which are suppressed by the prevailing views or attitudes in the life of a society gradually accumulate in the collective unconscious and activate its contents.

Certain individuals gifted with particularly strong intuition then become aware of the changes going on in it and translate these changes into communicable ideas. The new ideas spread rapidly because parallel changes have been taking place in the unconscious of other people. There is a general readiness to accept these new ideas, although on the other hand they often meet with violent resistance.

New ideas are not just the enemies of the old; they also appear as a rule in an extremely unacceptable form. (55)

When a problem that is at bottom personal, and therefore apparently subjective, coincides with external events that contain the same psychological elements as the personal conflict, it is suddenly transformed into a general question embracing the whole of society. In this way, the personal problem acquires a dignity it lacked hitherto, since a state of inner discord always has something humiliating and de-grading about it, so that one sinks into an ignominious con-dition both without and within, like a state dishonored by civil war.

It is this that makes one shrink from displaying before the public a purely personal conflict, provided of course that one does not suffer from an overdose of self-esteem. But if the connection between the personal problem and the larger contemporary events is discerned and understood, it brings release from the loneliness of the purely personal, and the subjective problem is magnified into a general question of our society. (56)

The tasks of every age differ, and it is only in retrospect that we can discern with certainty what had to be and what should not have been. In the momentary present, the con-flict of opinions will always rage, for "war is the father of all."

History alone decides the issue. Truth is not eternal—it is a program to be fulfilled. The more "eternal" a truth, the more lifeless it is and worthless; it says nothing more to us because it is self-evident. (56)

When something happens to a man and he supposes it to be personal only to himself, whereas, in reality, it is a quite universal experience, then his attitude is obviously wrong, too personal, and it tends to exclude him from human society. By the same token, we need to have not only a personal, contemporary consciousness, but also a supra-personal consciousness with a sense of historical continuity. (13)

The great events of world history are, at bottom, profoundly unimportant. In the last analysis, the essential thing is the life of the individual. This alone makes history, here alone do the great transformations first take place, and the whole future, the whole history of the world, ultimately spring as a gigantic summation from these hidden sources in individuals. In our most private and most subjective lives, we are not only the passive witnesses of our age, and its sufferers, but also its makers. (96)

# CREATIVITY, GENIUS, AND INNOVATION

The great trouble is that new ideas are rarely recognized by contemporaries. Most of them fight blindly all creative attempts in their special field. They thrive on things already known and therefore "safe." Universities are the worst in this respect. Yet one can find independent and intelligent personalities even among professors. (3)

To be "normal" is the ideal aim for the unsuccessful, for all those who are still below the general level of adaptation. But for people of more than average ability—people who have never found it difficult to gain success and to accomplish their share of the world's work—for them the moral compulsion to be nothing but normal signifies the bed of Procrustes—deadly and insupportable boredom, a hell of sterility and hopelessness. (51)

Whoever speaks in primordial images speaks with a thousand voices. He enthralls and overpowers, while at the same time, he lifts the idea he is seeking to express out of the occasional and the transitory into the realm of the everenduring. He transmutes our personal destiny into the destiny of humanity, and evokes in us all those beneficent forces that ever and anon have enabled humanity to find a refuge from every peril and to outlive the longest night. (46)

A great work of art is like a dream; for all the apparent obviousness, it does not explain itself and is always ambiguous. A dream never says "you ought" or "this is the truth." It presents an image in much the same way as nature allows a plant to grow, and it is up to us to draw conclusions.

If a person has a nightmare, it means he is either too much given to fear or too exempt from it; if he dreams of a wise old man, it means he is either too much of a pedant or else in need of a teacher. In a subtle way, both meanings come to the same thing, as we realize when we let a work of art act upon us as it has acted upon the artist. To grasp its meaning, we must allow it to shape us as it shaped him. Then we also understand the nature of his primordial experience.

He has plunged into the healing and redeeming depths of the collective psyche, where man is not lost in the isolation of consciousness and its errors and sufferings, but where all persons are caught in a common rhythm which allows the individual to communicate his feelings and strivings to humanity as a whole. (59)

Fantasy is not a sickness, but a natural and vital activity which helps the seeds of psychic development to grow. (93)

Creative life always stands outside convention. That is why, when the mere routine of life predominates in the form of convention and tradition, there is bound to be a destructive outbreak of creative energy. This outbreak is a catastrophe only when it is a mass phenomenon, but never in the individual who consciously submits to these higher powers and serves them with all his strength. (26)

Great innovations never come from above; they come invariably from below, just as trees never grow from the sky downward, but upward from the earth. The upheaval of our world and the upheaval of the unconscious are one and the same. (90)

Music certainly has to do with the collective unconscious, as drama does. This is evident in the music of Wagner, for example. Music expresses, in some way, the movement of the feelings—or emotional values—that cling to the unconscious processes. The nature of what happens in the collective unconscious is archetypal, and archetypes always have a numinous quality that expresses itself in emotional stress.

Music expresses in sounds what fantasies and visions express in visual images. I am not a musician and would not be able to develop these ideas for you in detail. I can only draw your attention to the fact that music represents the movement, development, and transformation of motifs of the collective unconscious. In Wagner, this is very clear, and also in Beethoven. (3)

Perhaps art has no "meaning," at least not as we understand meaning. Perhaps it is like Nature, which simply is and "means" nothing beyond that. Is "meaning" necessarily more than mere interpretation—an interpretation secreted into something by an intellect hungry for meaning? Art, it has been said, is beauty, and "a thing of beauty is a joy forever." It needs no meaning, for meaning has nothing to with art. (46)

The essence of a work of art is not to be found in the personal idiosyncrasies that creep into it—indeed, the more there are of them, the less it is a work of art—but in rising above the personal and speaking from the mind and heart of the artist to the mind and heart of humanity. The personal aspect of art is a limitation and even a vice. (59)

Personal causes have as much or as little to do with a work of art as the soil with the plant that springs from it. We can certainly learn to understand some of the plant's peculiarities by getting to know its habitat, and for the botanist, this is an important part of his equipment. But nobody will maintain that everything essential has then been discovered about the plant itself.

The personal orientation which the doctor needs when confronted with the question of etiology in medicine is quite out of place in dealing with a work of art, just because a work of art is not a human being, but is something suprapersonal. It is a thing and not a personality; hence, it cannot be judged by personal criteria. Indeed, the special significance of a true work of art resides in the fact that it has escaped from the limitations of the personal and has soared beyond the personal concerns of its creator. (46)

Every period has its bias, its particular prejudice, and its psychic malaise. An epoch is like an individual; it has its own limitations of conscious outlook, and therefore requires a compensatory adjustment. This is effected by the collective unconscious when a poet or seer lends expression to the unspoken desire of his times and shows the way, by word or deed, to its fulfillment: regardless whether this blind collective need results in good or evil, in the salvation of an epoch or its destruction. (59)

Out of a playful movement of elements whose interrelations are not immediately apparent, patterns arise which an observant and critical intellect can only evaluate afterwards. The creation of something new is not accomplished by the intellect, but the play instinct acting from inner necessity. The creative mind plays with the objects it loves. (56)

We know that every good idea and all creative work are the offspring of the imagination, and have their source in what one is pleased to call infantile fantasy. Not the artist alone but every creative individual whatsoever owes all that is greatest in his life to fantasy. (56)

The dynamic principle of fantasy is play, a characteristic also of the child, and as such it appears inconsistent with the principle of serious work. But without this playing with fantasy, no creative work has ever yet come to birth. The debt we owe to the play of imagination is incalculable. It is therefore short-sighted to treat fantasy, an account of its daring or objectionable nature, as a thing of little worth. (56)

The true genius nearly always intrudes and disturbs. He speaks to a temporal world out of a world eternal. He says the wrong things at the right time. Eternal truths are never true at any given moment in history. The process of transformation has to make a halt in order to digest and assimilate the utterly impractical things that the genius has produced from the storehouse of eternity. Yet the genius is the healer of his time, because anything he reveals of eternal truth is healing. (83)

A gift [often] develops in inverse ratio to the personality as a whole, and one has the impression that a creative personality grows at the expense of the human being. Sometimes, indeed, there is such a discrepancy between the genius and his human qualities that one has to ask oneself whether a little less talent might not have been better.

What after all is great talent beside moral inferiority? There are not a few gifted persons whose usefulness is paralyzed, not to say perverted, by their human shortcomings. A gift is not an absolute value, or rather, it is such a value only when the rest of the personality keeps pace with it. (32)

Art is a kind of innate drive that seizes a human being and makes him its instrument. The artist is not a person endowed with free will who seeks his own ends, but one who allows art to realize its purposes through him. As a human being, he may have moods and a will and personal aims, but as an artist, he is "man" in a higher sense—he is "collective man," a vehicle and molder of the unconscious psychic life of humanity. That is his office, and it is sometimes so heavy a burden that he is fated to sacrifice happiness and everything that makes life worth living for the ordinary human being. (59)

The normal man can follow the general trend without injury to himself; but the [person] who takes to the back streets and alleys because he cannot endure the broad highway will be the first to discover the psychic elements that are waiting to play their part in the life of the collective.

The artist's relative lack of adaptation turns out to his advantage: it enables him to follow his own yearnings far from the beaten path, and to discover what it is that would meet the unconscious needs of his age. Thus, just as the one-sidedness of the individual's conscious attitude is corrected by reactions from the unconscious, so art represents a process of self-regulation in the life of nations and epochs. (46)

This is the sickness of our modern artists, that they only paint or draw and reckon it a virtue to do anything rather than think, unlike the great artists of the Renaissance. I have always found it very difficult to discuss these problems with [artists today]. The greatness of the Renaissance artist lies not least in the fact that he worked with the whole of his personality, while the artist of today assiduously avoids anything meaningful. (3)

Aestheticism is not fitted to solve the exceedingly serious and difficult task of educating man, for it always presupposes the very thing it should create: the capacity to love beauty. It actually hinders a deeper investigation of the problem, because it always averts its face from anything evil, ugly, and difficult, and aims at pleasure, even though it be of an edifying kind. Aestheticism therefore lacks all moral force, because [at root], it is still only a refined hedonism. (56)

To rush ahead is to invite blows, and if you don't get them from the teacher, you will get them from fate, and generally from both. The gifted child will do well to accustom himself early to the fact that any excellence puts him in an exceptional position and exposes him to a great many risks, the chief of which is an exaggerated self-confidence. Against this the only protection is humility and obedience, and even these do not always work. (32)

The greatness of historical personalities has never lain in their abject submission *to* convention, but on the contrary, in their deliverance *from* convention. They tower up like mountain peaks above the mass that still clung to its collective fears, its beliefs, laws, and systems, and boldly choose their own way.

To the man on the street, it has always seemed miraculous that anyone should turn aside from the beaten track with its known destinations, and strike out on the steep and narrow path leading into the unknown. Hence, it was always believed that such a man, if not actually crazy, was possessed by a daemon or a god; for the miracle of a man being able to act otherwise than as humanity has always acted could be explained only by the gift of daemonic power or divine spirit. (26)

A person must pay dearly for the divine gift of creative fire. It is as though each of us was born with a limited store of energy. In the artist, the strongest force in his makeup, that is, his creativeness, will seize and all but monopolize this energy, leaving so little over that nothing of value can come of it.

The creative impulse can drain him of his humanity to such a degree that the personal ego can exist only on a primitive or inferior level and is driven to develop all sorts of defects—ruthlessness, selfishness, vanity, and other infantile traits. These inferiorities are the only means by which it can maintain its vitality and prevent itself from being wholly depleted. (59)

New ideas, if they are not just a flash in the pan, generally require at least a generation to take root. Psychological innovations probably take much longer, since in this field more than in any other, practically everybody sets himself up as an authority. (81)

Widely accepted ideas are never the personal property of their so-called author. On the contrary, he is the bondservant of his ideas. Impressive ideas which are hailed as truths have something peculiar about them. Although they come into being at a definite time, they are and have always been timeless. They arise from that realm of creative psychic life out of which the ephemeral mind of the single human being grows like a plant that blossoms, bears fruit and seed, and then withers and dies. Ideas spring from something greater than the personal human being. Man does not make his ideas; we could say that man's ideas make him. (30)

The time is as great as one thinks, and man grows to the stature of the time. (37)

Certain people make history and others build a little house in the suburbs. (4)

Many artists, philosophers, and even scientists owe some of their best ideas to inspirations that appear suddenly from the unconscious. We can find clear proof of this fact in the history of science itself.

For example, the French mathematician Poincaré and the chemist Kekule owed important scientific discoveries, as they themselves admit, to sudden pictorial "revelations" from the unconscious. The so-called "mystical" experience of the French philosopher Descartes involved a similar, sudden revelation in which he saw in a flash of light the "order of all sciences." The British author Robert Louis Stevenson had spent years looking for a story that would fit his "strong sense of man's double being" when the plot of *Dr. Jekyll and Mr. Hyde* was suddenly revealed to him in a dream.

It is true that there are unprofitable, futile, morbid and unsatisfying fantasies whose sterile nature is immediately recognized in every person endowed with common sense; but the faulty performance proves nothing against the normal performance. All the works of humanity have their origin in creative imagination. (94)

The psyche creates reality every day. The only expression I can use for this activity is *fantasy*. Fantasy is just as much feeling as thinking, as much intuition as sensation. There is no psychic function that, through fantasy, is not inextricably bound up with the other psychic functions. Sometimes it appears in primordial form, sometimes it is the ultimate and boldest product of all our faculties combined.

Fantasy, therefore, seems to me the clearest expression of the specific activity of the psyche. It is pre-eminently the creative activity from which the answers to all answerable questions come: it is the mother of all possibilities, where, like all psychological opposites, the inner and outer worlds are joined together in living union. (56)

The creative process, so far as we are able to follow it at all, consists in the unconscious activation of an archetypal image, and in elaborating and shaping this image into the finished work. By giving it shape, the artist translates it into the language of the present, and so makes it possible for us to find our way back to the deepest springs of life.

Therein lies the social significance of art: it is constantly at work educating the spirit of the age, conjuring up the forms in which the age is most lacking. The unsatisfied yearning of the artist reaches back to the primordial image in the unconscious which is best suited to compensate the inadequacy and one-sidedness of the present.

The artist seizes on this image, and in raising it from the

deepest unconsciousness, he brings it into relation with conscious values, thereby transforming it until it can be accepted by the minds of his contemporaries according to their powers. (46)

It is the duty of one who goes his own way to inform society of what he finds on his voyage of discovery, be it cooling water for the thirsty or the sandy wastes of unfruitful error. Not the criticism of individual contemporaries will decide the truth or falsity of his discoveries but future generations. There are things that are not yet true today; perhaps we dare not find them true, but tomorrow they may be.

So every man whose fate is to go his individual way, must proceed with hopefulness and watchfulness, ever conscious of his loneliness and its dangers. (81)

# LOVE, SEX, AND INTIMACY

Whatever I say [about romantic love] is a general rule which shouldn't be recklessly generalized. Man is a most peculiar experiment of nature and particularly in erotic respects simply anything is possible. (3)

Where love reigns, there is no will to power; and where the will to power is paramount, love is lacking. The one is but the shadow of the other. (81)

The love problem is part of humanity's heavy toll of suffering, and nobody should be ashamed of having to pay his tribute. (15)

Man is not only governed by the sex instinct; there are other instincts as well. For instance, in biology you can see that the nutritional instinct is just as important as the sex instinct, although in primitive societies sexuality plays a role much smaller than food. Food is the all-important interest and desire. Sex—that is something they can have everywhere—they are not shy. But food is difficult to obtain, and so it is the main interest.

Then in other societies—I mean civilized societies—the power drive plays a much greater role than sex. For instance, there are many big businessmen who are impotent because their full energy is going into moneymaking or dictating the laws to everybody else. That is much more interesting to them than affairs with women. (1)

Every man carries within him the eternal image of woman, not the image of this or that particular woman, but a definitive feminine image. This image is fundamentally unconscious, an hereditary factor of primordial origin engraved in the living organic system of the man, an imprint or "archetype" of all the ancestral experiences of the female: a deposit, as it were, of all the impressions ever made by woman. . . . Since this image is unconscious, it is always unconsciously projected upon the person of the beloved, and is one of the chief reasons for passionate attraction or aversion. (6)

In its primary, "unconscious" form, the *animus* is a compound of spontaneous, unpremeditated opinions which exercise a powerful influence on the woman's emotional life, while the *anima* is similarly compounded of feelings which thereafter influence or distort the man's understanding ("She has turned his head"). Consequently, the *animus* likes to project itself upon "intellectuals" and all kinds of "heroes" including tenors, artists, and sporting celebrities. The *anima* has a predilection for everything that is unconscious, dark, equivocal, and unrelated in woman, and also for her vanity, frigidity, and helplessness. (6)

It takes much energy to be in love. In America, you give so many opportunities both to your men and women that they do not save any of their vital force for loving. (2)

You believe, for instance, that American marriages are the happiest in the world. I say they are the most tragic. I know this not only from study of the people as a whole, but from my study of the individuals who come to me. I find that the men and women are giving their vital energy to everything except to the relation between themselves. In that relation, all is confusion. The women are the mothers of their husbands as well as of their children, yet at the same time, there is in them the old, old primitive desire to be possessed, to yield, to surrender. And there is nothing in the man for her to surrender to except his kindness, his courtesy, his generosity, his chivalry. His competitor, his rival in business, must yield but she need not. (2)

You have experienced in your marriage what is an almost universal fact: that individuals are different from one another. Basically, each remains for the other an unfathomable enigma. There is never complete concord. If you have committed a mistake at all, it consisted in having striven too hard to understand your wife completely and not reckoning with the fact that, in the end, people don't want to know what secrets are slumbering in their souls.

If you struggle too much to penetrate into another person, you find that you have thrust him into a defensive position, and resistances develop because, through your efforts to penetrate and understand, he feels forced to examine those things in himself which he doesn't want to examine. Everybody has his dark side which—so long as all goes well—he had better not know about. (3)

I find it incomprehensible how anybody can credit me with being opposed to female suffrage out of fear that it might lead to the danger of "masculinization." My experience has impressed me with the tenacity and toughness of the female nature, which nothing has changed for thousands of years, far too deeply upon me for me to suppose that the right to vote could bring such a wonder to pass. Naturally, political activity can masculinize a woman, but so can all other activities: for instance, wives and mothers who, in the common estimation could have a satisfying fate in their feminine role tyrannize over husbands and families with a masculine animus who can throw his weight about without any need on their part to have the right to vote as well. In an utterly feminine way, a woman can have a—from her point of view—well-founded opinion without suffering the slightest injury to her nature. The fact that she can have convictions and insights is a generally human characteristic, and one that is not peculiar only to men.

At all times, there have been wise and shrewd women to whom even clever men have gone for advice. There are countless women who succeed in public life without losing their femininity. On the contrary, they succeeded precisely because of it. The unpleasant power-complex of the female animus is encountered only when a woman does not allow her feeling to express itself naturally or handles it in an inferior way. But this can happen in all situations of life and has nothing whatever to do with the right to vote. (3)

It is hard to believe that this teeming world is too poor to provide an object for human loves—it offers boundless opportunities to everyone.

It is rather the inability to love which robs a person of these opportunities. The world is empty only to him who does not know how to direct his libido towards things and people, and to render them alive and beautiful.

What compels us to create a substitute from within ourselves is not an external lack, but our own inability to include anything outside ourselves in our love. Certainly the difficulties and adversities of the struggle for existence may oppress us, yet even the worst conditions need not hinder love. On the contrary, they often spur us on to greater efforts. (78)

In spite of all indignant protestations to the contrary, the fact remains that love—using the word in the wider sense which belongs to it by right and embraces more than sexuality—its problems and its conflicts, is of fundamental importance in human life and, as careful inquiry consistently shows, is of far greater significance than the individual suspects. (81)

Our civilization enormously underestimates the importance of sexuality, but just because of the repressions imposed upon it, sexuality breaks through into every conceivable field where it does not belong, and uses such an indirect mode of expression that we may expect to meet it all of a sudden practically everywhere.

Thus, the very idea of an intimate understanding of the human psyche, which is actually a very pure and beautiful thing, becomes besmirched and perversely distorted by the intrusion of an indirect sexual meaning. A direct and spontaneous expression of sexuality is a natural occurrence and, as such, never ugly or repulsive. It is "moral" repression that makes sexuality on the one hand dirty and hypocritical, and on the other, shameless and blatant. (78)

Nowadays we have no real sexual morality, only a legislated attitude toward sexuality, just as the Middle Ages had no real morality of money-making, but only prejudices and a legalistic viewpoint. We are not yet far enough advanced to distinguish between moral and immoral behavior in the realm of free sexual activity.

This is clearly expressed in the customary treatment, or rather ill-treatment, of unmarried mothers. All the repulsive hypocrisy, the high tide of prostitution and of venereal diseases, we owe to the barbarous, wholesale legal condemnation of certain kinds of sexual behavior, and to our inability to develop a fine moral sense for the enormous psychological differences that exist in the domain of free sexual activity. (71)

Normal sex life, as a shared experience with apparently similar aims, further strengthens the feeling of unity and identity. This state is described as one of complete harmony, and is extolled as a great happiness ("one heart and one soul") not without good reason. . . . It is, in truth, a genuine and incontestable experience of the divine, whose transcendent force obliterates and consumes everything individual: a real communion with life and the impersonal power of fate. (39)

Most of what men say about feminine eroticism, and particularly about the emotional life of women, is derived from their own anima projections and distorted accordingly. (39)

It you take a typical intellectual who is terribly afraid of falling in love, you will think his fear very foolish. . . . But [such men] are right to be afraid, because their undoing will be in their feeling. Nobody can attack them in their intellect. There they are strong and can stand alone, but in their feelings they can be influenced, they can be caught, they can be cheated, and they know it. Therefore, never force a man into his feeling when he is an intellectual. He controls it with an iron hand because it is very dangerous. (4)

Human relationship leads into the world of the psyche, into that intermediate realm between sense and spirit, which contains something of both and yet forfeits nothing of its own unique character. (86)

Our unwillingness to see our own faults and the projection of them onto others is the source of most quarrels, and the strongest guarantee that injustice, animosity, and persecution will not easily die out. (25)

Relationship is possible only if there is a psychic distance between people, in the same way that morality presupposes freedom. (86)

The real existence of an enemy upon whom one can foist off everything evil is an enormous relief to one's conscience. You can then at least say, without hesitation, who the devil is: you are quite certain that the cause of your misfortune is outside, and not in your own attitude. (31)

Most men are erotically blinded—they commit the unpardonable mistake of confusing Eros with sex. A man thinks he possesses a woman if he has her sexually. He never possesses her less, for to a woman the Eros-relationship is the real and decisive one. For her, marriage is a relationship with sex thrown in as an accompaniment. (86)

Traditionally, the man is regarded as the marriage-breaker. This legend comes from times long past, when men still had leisure to pursue all sorts of pastimes. But today life makes so many demands on men that the noble hidalgo, Don Juan, is to be seen nowhere save in the theater. More than ever, man loves his comfort, for ours is an age of neurasthenia, impotence, and easy chairs. There is no energy left for window-climbing and duels.

If anything is to happen in the way of adultery, it must not be too difficult. In no respect must it cost too much; hence the adventure can only be of a transitory kind. The man of today is thoroughly scared of jeopardizing marriage as an institution. (86)

Seldom or never does a marriage develop into an individual relationship smoothly and without crises. There is no birth of consciousness without pain. (39)

Eros is a questionable fellow and will always remain so, whatever the legislation of the future may have to say about it. He belongs on one side to man's primordial animal nature which will endure as long as man has an animal body. On the other side, he is related to the highest forms of the spirit. But he only thrives when spirit and instinct are in right harmony.

If one or the other aspect is lacking in him, the result is injury or at least a lopsidedness that may easily veer toward the pathological. Too much of the animal distorts the civilized man, too much civilization makes sick animals. (81)

The conflict between ethics and sex today is not just a collision between instinctuality and morality, but a struggle to give an instinct its rightful place in our lives, and to recognize in this instinct a power which seeks expression and evidently may not be trifled with, and therefore cannot be made to fit with our well-meaning moral laws.

Sexuality is not mere instinctuality; it is an indisputably creative power that is not only the basic cause of our individual lives, but a very serious factor in our psychic life as well. Today we know only too well the grave consequences that sexual disturbances can bring in their train. (45)

There are rather serious misgivings as to whether our existing moral views have dealt fairly with the nature of sex. From this doubt, there naturally arises a legitimate interest in any attempt to understand the nature of sex more truly and deeply. (45)

We could call sexuality the spokesman of the instincts, which is why from the spiritual standpoint sex is the chief antagonist, not because sexual indulgence is in itself more immoral than excessive eating and drinking, avarice, tyranny, and other extravagances, but because the spirit senses in sexuality a counterpart equal and indeed akin to itself.

For just as the spirit would press sexuality, like every other instinct, into its service, so sexuality has an ancient claim upon the spirit, which it once—in procreation, pregnancy, birth, and childhood—contained within itself, and whose passion the spirit can never dispense with in its creations. (45)

The optimism of life is not to be found in crude egoism, for fundamentally man is so constituted that the pleasure he gives his neighbor is something essential to him. Nor can the optimism be reached by an unbridled craving for individualist supremacy, for the collective element in man is so powerful that his longing for fellowship would destroy all pleasure in naked egoism.

The optimum can be reached only through obedience to the tidal laws of the libido, by which systole alternates with diastole—laws which bring pleasure and the necessary limitations of pleasure, and also set us those individual life-tasks without whose accomplishment the vital optimism can never be attained. (56)

All dreams reveal spiritual experiences, provided one does not apply one's own point of view to the interpretation of them. Freud says that all man's longings expressed in his dreams relate to sexuality. It is true that man is a being with sex. But he is also a being with a stomach and a liver. As well say that because he has a liver all his troubles come from that one organ.

Primitive man has little difficulty with sex. The fulfillment of his sexual desires is too easy to constitute a problem. What concerns primitive man—and I have lived among primitives, and Freud has not—is his *food:* where he is to get it, and enough of it.

Civilized man in his dreams reveals his spiritual need. (2)

We understand another person in the same way as we understand, or seek to understand, ourselves. What we do not understand in ourselves, we do not understand in the other person, either. So there is plenty to ensure that his image will be for the most part subjective. As we know, even an intimate friendship is no guarantee of objective knowledge. (31)

# THE ART OF PSYCHOTHERAPY

You can learn a great deal of psychology through studying books, but you will find that this psychology is not very helpful in practical life. A [person] entrusted with the care of souls ought to have a certain wisdom of life which does not consist of words only, but chiefly of experience. Such psychology, as I understand it, is not only a piece of knowledge, but a certain wisdom of life at the same time. If such a thing can be taught at all, it must be in the way of a personal experience of the human soul. Such an experience is possible only when the teaching has a personal character, namely when you are personally taught and not generally. (3)

The greatest mistake an analyst can make is to assume that his patient has a psychology similar to his own. (31)

Anyone who wants to know the human psyche will learn next to nothing from experimental psychology. He would be better advised to put away his scholar's gown, bid farewell to his study, and wander with human heart through the world.

There, in the horrors of prisons, lunatic asylums and hospitals, in drab suburban pubs, in brothels and gambling-hells, in the salons of the elegant, the Stock Exchanges, Socialist meetings, churches, revivalist gatherings and ecstatic sects, through love and hate, through the experience of passion in every form in his own body, he would reap richer stores of knowledge than textbooks a foot thick could give him, and he will know how to doctor the sick with real knowledge of the human soul. (91)

Experience has taught me to keep away from therapeutic "methods" as much as from diagnoses. The enormous variation among individuals and their neuroses has set before me the ideal of approaching each case with a minimum of prior assumptions. The ideal would naturally be to have no assumptions at all. But this is impossible even if one exercises the most rigorous self-criticism, for one is *oneself* the biggest of all one's assumptions, and the one with the gravest consequences.

Try as we may to have no assumptions and to use no ready-made methods, the assumption that *I myself am* will determine my method: as I am, so will I proceed. (68)

It is enough to drive one to despair that in practical psychology there are no universally valid recipes and rules. There are only individual cases with the most heterogeneous needs and demands—so heterogeneous that we can virtually never know in advance what course a given case will take, for which reason it is better for the doctor to abandon all preconceived opinions.

This does not mean that he should throw them overboard, but that in any given case he should use them merely as hypotheses for a possible explanation. (51)

Medicine in the hand of a fool was ever poison and death. Just as we demand from a surgeon, besides his technical knowledge, a skilled hand, courage, presence of mind, and power of decision, so we must expect from an analyst a very serious and thorough psychoanalytic training of his own personality before we are willing to entrust a patient to him.

I would even go so far as to say that the acquisition and practice of the psychoanalytic technique presuppose not only a specific psychological gift, but in the very first place, a serious concern with the molding of one's own character. (79)

The object of therapy is not the neurosis but the man who has the neurosis. We have long known, for instance, that a cardiac nervous neurosis comes not from the heart, as old medical mythology would have it, but from the mind of the sufferer. Nor does it come from some obscure corner of the unconscious, as many psychotherapists still struggle to believe; it comes from the totality of a man's life and from all the experiences that have accumulated over the years and decades, and finally, not merely from his life as an individual, but from his psychic experience within the family or even the social group. (75)

An analyst can help his patient just so far as he himself has gone and not a step further. In my practice, I have had from the beginning to deal with patients who got "stuck" with their previous analysis, and this always happened at the point where the analyst could make no further progress with himself. (68)

Unfortunately far too many of us talk about a man only as it would be desirable for him to be, never about the man as he really is. But the doctor has always to do with the real man, who remains obstinately himself until all sides of his reality are recognized. True education can only start from naked reality, not from a delusive ideal. (81)

We cannot demand of our patients a faith which they do reject because they do not understand it, or which does not suit them even though we may hold it ourselves. We have to rely on the curative powers inherent in the patient's own nature, regardless of whether the ideas that emerge agree with any known creed or philosophy. (69)

The small world of the child, the family milieu, is the model for the big world. The more intensely the family sets its stamp on the child, the more he will be emotionally inclined, as an adult, to see in the great world his former small world.

Of course, this must not be taken as a conscious intellectual process. On the contrary, the patient feels and sees the difference between now and then, and tries as well as he can to adapt himself. Perhaps he will even believe himself perfectly adapted, since he may be able to grasp the situation intellectually, but that does not prevent his emotions from lagging far behind his intellectual insight. (79)

No psychotherapist should lack that natural reserve which prevents people from riding roughshod over mysteries they do not understand and trampling them flat. This reserve will enable him to pull back in good time when he encounters the mystery of the patient's difference from himself, and to avoid the danger—unfortunately only too real—of committing psychic murder in the name of therapy.

For the ultimate cause of a neurosis is something *positive* which needs to be safeguarded for the patient; otherwise he suffers a psychic loss, and the result of the treatment is at best a defective cure. (68)

It is presumptuous to think that we can always say what is good or bad for the patient. Perhaps he knows something is really bad and does it anyway, and then gets a bad conscience. From the therapeutic, that is to say empirical, point of view, this may be very good indeed for him. Perhaps he *has* to experience the power of evil and suffer accordingly, because only in that way can he give up his Pharisaic attitude to other people.

Perhaps fate or the unconscious or God—call it what you will—had to give him a hard knock and roll him in the dirt, because only such a drastic experience could strike home, pull him out of his infantilism, and make him more mature. How can anyone find out how much he needs to be saved if he is quite sure that there is nothing he needs saving from? (33)

It is a very difficult and important question, what you call the technique of dealing with the shadow. There is, as a matter of fact, no technique at all, inasmuch as technique means that there is a known and perhaps even prescribable way to deal with a certain difficulty or task.

There is, for instance, no particular technique that would help us to reconcile two political parties opposing each other. It can be a question of good will, or diplomatic cunning or civil war, or anything. If one can speak of a technique at all, it consists solely in an attitude. First of all, one has to accept and to take seriously into account the existence of the shadow. Secondly, it is necessary to be informed about its qualities and intentions. Thirdly, long and difficult negotiations will be unavoidable. (3)

Anybody whose calling it is to guide souls should have his own soul guided first, so that he knows what it means to deal with the human soul. Knowing your own darkness is the best method for dealing with the darkness of other people. It would not help you very much to study books only, though it is indispensable too. But it would help you most to have a personal insight into the secrets of the human soul. Otherwise, everything remains a clever intellectual trick, consisting of empty words and leading to empty talk. You may try to find out what I mean in my books and if you have a close friend, try to look behind his screen in order to discover yourself. That would be a good beginning. (3)

When a crack runs through a house, the entire building is affected and not merely one half of it. The house is no longer as trustworthy as before. A conscientious builder does not try to convince the owner that the rooms on either side of the crack are still in an excellent condition, but will set to work on the crack and seek ways and means to mend it. The splendid and costly furnishings of the rooms will interest him only in so far as he is intent on saving the rooms. He has no time to wander around admiringly, exclaiming that they are the most beautiful in the world, when there is already a creaking in the beams.

As a doctor, I am interested in only one thing: how can the wound be healed? (3)

When a patient complains that he knows exactly what to do, I say: "Well, you are in the position of everybody who knows what he might do." He has now to set to work to do at least something of it and to find out how to do it. There would be no difficulty in life if one always knew beforehand how to do a thing. Life is some sort of art and not a straight rail or a ready-made product to be had at every corner. (3)

It is a remarkable thing about psychotherapy: you cannot learn any recipes by heart and then apply them more-or-less suitably, but can cure only from one central point, and that consists in understanding the patient as a psychological whole and approaching him as a human being, leaving aside all theory and listening attentively to whatever he has to say. Even a thorough discussion can work wonders. It is, of course, essential for the psychotherapist to have a fair knowledge of himself, for anyone who does not understand himself cannot understand others and can never be psychotherapeutically effective unless he has first treated himself with the same medicine. (3)

Sometimes one is apparently quite aware of one's projections though one does not know their full extent. And that portion of which one is not aware remains unconscious and still appears as if belonging to the object. This often happens in practical analysis.

You say, for instance: "Now, look here, you simply project the image of your father onto that man, or into myself," and you assume that this is a perfectly satisfactory explanation and quite sufficient to dissolve the projection. It is satisfactory to the doctor, perhaps, but not to the patient. Because, if there is still something more in that projection, the patient will keep on projecting. (4)

It is obvious that in the course of his practice, a doctor will come across people who have a great effect on him. He meets personalities who, for better or worse, never stir the interest of the public and who nevertheless, or for that very reason, possess unusual qualities, or whose destiny is to pass through unprecedented developments and disasters.

Sometimes they are persons of extraordinary talents, who might well inspire another to give his life for them; but these talents may be implanted in so strangely unfavorable a psychic disposition that we cannot tell whether it is a question of genius or of fragmentary development.

Frequently, too, in this unlikely soil, there flower rare blossoms of the psyche which we would never have thought to find in the flatlands of society. For psychotherapy to be effective, a close rapport is needed, so close that the doctor cannot shut his eyes to the heights and depths of human suffering.

The rapport consists, after all, in a constant comparison and mutual comprehension, in the dialectical confrontation of two opposing psychic realities. If for some reason these mutual impressions do not impinge on each other, the psychotherapeutic process remains ineffective, and no change is produced. Unless both doctor and patient become a problem to each other, no solution is found. (6)

Freud's greatest achievement probably consisted in taking neurotic patients seriously and entering into their peculiar individual psychology. He had the courage to let the case material speak for itself, and in this way was able to penetrate into the real psychology of his patients. He saw with the patient's eyes, so to speak, and so reached a deeper understanding of mental illness than had hitherto been possible. In this respect, he was free of bias, courageous, and succeeded in overcoming a host of prejudices.

Like an Old Testament prophet, he undertook to overthrow false gods, to rip the veils away from a mass of dishonesties and hypocrisies, mercilessly exposing the rottenness of the contemporary psyche. He did not falter in the face of the unpopularity such an enterprise entailed. The impetus which he gave to our civilization sprang from his discovery of an avenue to the unconscious.

By evaluating dreams as the most important source of information concerning the unconscious processes, he gave back to mankind a tool that had seemed irretrievably lost. He demonstrated empirically the presence of an unconscious psyche which had hitherto existed only as a philosophical postulate. (6)

Together the patient and I address ourselves to the 2,000,000-year-old man that is in all of us. In the last analysis, most of our difficulties come from losing contact with our instincts, with the age-old unforgotten wisdom stored up in us. And where do we make contact with this old man in us? In our dreams. (9)

Never apply any theory, but always ask the patient how he feels about his dream images. For dreams are always about a particular problem of the individual about which he has a wrong conscious judgment. The dreams are the reaction to our unconscious attitude in the same way that the body reacts when we overeat or do not eat enough or when we ill-treat it in some other way. Dreams are the natural reaction of the self-regulating psychic system. (4)

We always find in the patient a conflict which at a certain point is connected with the great problems of society. Hence, when the analysis is pushed to this point, the apparently individual conflict of the patient is revealed as a universal conflict of his environment and epoch.

Neurosis is nothing less than an individual attempt, however unsuccessful, to solve a universal problem: indeed, it cannot be otherwise, for a general problem, a "question," is not an [issue] per se, but exists only in the hearts of individuals. (4)

We cannot change anything unless we accept it. Condemnation does not liberate, it oppresses. I am the oppressor of the person I condemn, not his friend and fellow-sufferer. I do not in the least mean to say that we must never pass judgment when we desire to help and improve. But if the doctor wishes to help a human being, he must be able to accept him as he is. And he can do this in reality only when he has already seen and accepted himself as he is. (64)

Healing comes only from what leads the [individual] beyond himself and beyond his entanglements in the ego. (49)

When I am treating a man, I must be exceedingly careful not to knock him down with my views or my personality, because he has to fight his lonely fight through life and he must be able to trust in his perhaps very incomplete armor and in his own perhaps very imperfect aim.

When I say, "That is not good and should be better," I deprive him of courage. He must plough his field with a plough that is not good perhaps; mine may be better, but what good is it to him? He has not got my plough. I have it, and he cannot borrow it. He must use his own perhaps very incomplete tools and has to work with his own inherited capacities, whatever they are. (5)

In our time, which puts so much weight on the socialization of the individual because a special capacity for adaptation is also needed, the formation of psychologically-oriented groups is certainly more important than ever. But in view of the notorious tendency of people to lean on others and cling to various –isms instead of finding security and independence within themselves, which is the prime requisite, there is a danger that the individual will equate the group with father and mother and so remain just as dependent, insecure, and infantile as before. He may become adapted socially, but what of his individuality, which alone gives meaning to the social fabric?

I have reached the following conclusions:

1. Group therapy is indispensable for the education of the social human being.
2. It is not a substitute for individual analysis.
3. The two forms of psychotherapy complement each other.
4. The danger of group therapy is getting stuck on the collective level.
5. The danger of individual analysis is the neglect of social adaptation. (3)

An ancient adept has said, "If the wrong man uses the right means, the right means work in the wrong way." This Chinese saying, unfortunately only too true, stands in sharp contrast to our belief in the "right" method irrespective of the man who applies it.

In reality, everything depends on the man and little or nothing on the method. (84)

## RELIGION, MYTH, AND PHILOSOPHY

Can you imagine a real prophet or savior in our days of television and press reportage? He would perish by his own popularity within a few weeks. (3)

Everything to do with religion, everything it is and asserts, touches the human soul so closely that psychology least of all can afford to overlook it. (53)

God always speaks mythologically. (3)

Whoever speaks of the reality of the soul or psyche is accused of "psychologism." Psychology is spoken of as if it were "only" psychology and nothing else. The notion that there can be psychic factors which correspond to the divine figures is regarded as a devaluation of the latter. It smacks of blasphemy to think that a religious experience is a psychic process; for, so it is argued, a religious experience "is not *only* psychological." Anything psychic is only Nature and therefore, people think, nothing religious can come out of it.

At the same time, such critics never hesitate to derive all religions—with the exception of their own—from the nature of the psyche. (58)

So far mythologies have always helped themselves out with solar, lunar, meteorological, vegetal, and other ideas of the kind. The fact that myths are first and foremost psychic phenomena that reveal the nature of the soul is something they have absolutely refused to see until now. Primitive man is not much interested in objective explanations of the obvious, but he has an imperative need—or rather, his unconscious psyche has an irresistible urge—to assimilate all outer sense experiences to inner, psychic events.

It is not enough for the primitive to see the sun rise and set; this external observation must at the same time be a psychic happening: the sun in its course must represent the fate of a god or hero who, in the last analysis, dwells nowhere except in the soul of man.

All the mythologized processes of nature, such as summer and winter, the phases of the moon, the rainy seasons, and so forth, are in no sense allegories of these objective occurrences. Rather, they are symbolic expressions of the inner, unconscious drama of the psyche which becomes accessible to man's unconscious by way of projection—that is, mirrored in the events of nature. (19)

What is the use of a religion without a mythos, since religion means, if anything at all, precisely that function which links us back to the eternal myth? (17)

The word "belief" is a difficult thing for me. I don't believe. I must have a reason for a certain hypothesis. Either I *know* a thing, and then I know it—I don't need to believe it. (7)

Great as is the value of Zen Buddhism for understanding the religious transformational process, its use among

Western people is very problematical. The mental education necessary for Zen is lacking in the West. Who among us would place such implicit trust in a superior Master and his incomprehensible ways?

The respect for the greater human personality is to be found only in the East. Could any of us boast that he believes in the possibility of a boundlessly paradoxical transformational experience, to the extent, moreover, of sacrificing many years of his life to the wearisome pursuit of such a goal?

And finally, who would dare to take upon himself the authority for such an unorthodox transformational experience—except a man who was little to be trusted, one who, maybe for pathological reasons, has too much to say for himself? Just such a person would have no cause to complain of any lack of following among us.

But let a "Master" set us a hard task, which requires more than mere parrot-talk, and the European begins to have doubts, for the steep path of self-development is to him as mournful and gloomy as the path to hell. (77)

Why is psychology the youngest of the empirical sciences? Why have we not long since discovered the unconscious and raised up its treasure-house of eternal images? Simply because we had a religious formula for everything psychic—and one that is far more beautiful and comprehensive than immediate experience. Though the Christian view of the world has paled for many people, the symbolic treasure-rooms of the East are still full of marvels that can nourish for a long time to come the passions for show and new clothes.

What is more, these images—be they Christian or Buddhist, or what you will—are lovely, mysterious, richly intuitive. Naturally, the more familiar we are with them, the more does constant usage polish them smooth, so that what remains is only banal superficiality and meaningless paradox. (19)

The myth of the hero . . . is first and foremost a self-representation of the longing of the unconscious, of its unquenched and unquenchable desire for the light of consciousness. But consciousness, continually in danger of being led astray by its own light and of becoming a rootless will o' the wisp, longs for the healing power of Nature, for the deep wells of being and for unconscious communion with life in all its countless forms. (78)

Modern man has heard enough about guilt and sin. He is sorely enough beset by his own bad conscience, and wants rather to know how he is best to reconcile himself with his own nature: how he is to love the enemy in his own heart and call the wolf his brother. (64)

Reverence for the great mysteries of nature, which the language of religion seeks to express in symbols hallowed by their antiquity, profound significance, and beauty, will not suffer from the extension of psychology to this domain, to which science has hitherto found no access. We only shift the symbols back a little, shedding a little light on their darker reaches, but without succumbing to the erroneous notion that we have created more than merely a new symbol for the same enigma that perplexed all ages before us. (56)

To gain an understanding of religious matters, probably all that is left us today is the psychological approach. That is why I take these thought-forms that have become historically fixed, try to melt them down again and pour them into molds of immediate experience. It is certainly a difficult undertaking to discover connecting links between dogma and immediate experience of psychological archetypes, but a study of the natural symbols of the unconscious gives us the necessary raw material. (60)

The gods of Greece and Rome perished from the same disease as did our Christian symbols: people discovered then, as today, that they had no thoughts whatever on the subject. On the other hand, the gods of the strangers still had unexhausted manna. Their names were weird and incomprehensible and their deeds portentously dark—something altogether different from the hackneyed *chronique scandaleuse* of Olympics.

At least one couldn't understand the Asiatic symbols, and for this reason they were not banal like the conventional gods. The fact that people accepted the new as unthinkingly as they had rejected the old did not become a problem at that time. Is it becoming a problem today?

Shall we be able to put on, like a new suit of clothes, ready-made symbols grown on foreign soil, saturated with foreign blood, spoken in a foreign tongue, nourished by a foreign culture, interwoven with foreign history, and so resemble a beggar who wraps himself in kingly raiment, a king who disguises himself as a beggar?

No doubt this is possible. Or is there something in our selves that commands us to go in for no mummeries, but perhaps to sew our garment ourselves? (19)

Anyone who has lost the historical symbols and cannot be satisfied with substitutes is certainly in a very difficult position today: before him there yawns the void, and he turns away from it in horror. What is worse, the vacuum gets filled with absurd political and social ideas, which one and all are distinguished by their spiritual bleakness. But if he cannot get along with these pedantic dogmatisms, he seems himself forced to be serious for once with his alleged trust in God, though it usually turns out that his fear of things going wrong if he did so is even more persuasive. (17)

It is not storms, not thunder and lightning, not rain and cloud that remain as images in the psyche, but the fantasies caused by the affects they arouse. I once experienced a violent earthquake, and my first, immediate feeling was that I no longer stood on the solid and familiar earth, but on the skin of a gigantic animal that was heaving under my feet. It was this image that impressed itself on me, not the physical fact.

Man's curses against devastating thunderstorms, his terror of the unchained elements—these affects anthropomorphize the passion of nature, and the purely physical element becomes an angry god. (76)

It does not surprise me that psychology debouches into philosophy, for the thinking that underlies philosophy is after all a psychic activity which, as such, is the proper study of psychology. I always think of psychology as encompassing the whole of the psyche, and that includes philosophy and theology and many other things besides. For underlying all philosophies and all religions are the facts of the human soul, which may ultimately be the arbiters of truth and error. (31)

The physical world and the perceptual world are two very different things. Knowing this we have no encouragement whatever to think that our metaphysical picture of the world corresponds to the transcendental reality. Moreover, the statements made about the latter are so boundlessly varied that with the best of intentions we cannot know who is right.

The denominational religions recognized this long ago and in consequence each of them claims that it is the only true one and, on top of this, that it is not merely a human truth but the truth directly inspired and revealed by God. Every theologian speaks simply of "God," by which he intends it to be understood that his "god" is *the* God. But one speaks of the paradoxical God of the Old Testament, another of the incarnate God of Love, a third of the God who has a heavenly bride, and so on, and each criticizes the other but never himself. (41)

Although the actual moment of conversion often seems quite sudden and unexpected, we know from experience that such a fundamental upheaval always requires a long period of incubation. It is only when this preparation is complete, that is to say when the individual is ripe for conversion, that the new insight breaks through with violent emotion.

Saul, as he was then called, had unconsciously been a Christian for a long time, and this would explain his fanatical hatred of the Christians, because fanaticism is always found in those who have to stifle a secret doubt. That is why converts are always the worst fanatics. (55)

People who merely believe and don't think always forget that they continually expose themselves to their own worst enemy: doubt. Wherever belief reigns, doubt lurks in the background. But thinking people welcome doubt; it serves them as a valuable stepping-stone to better knowledge.

People who can believe should be a little more tolerant of their fellows who are only capable of thinking. Belief has already conquered the summit which thinking tries to win by toilsome climbing. The believer ought not to project his habitual enemy, doubt, upon the thinker, thereby suspecting him of destructive designs. (53)

The more unconscious we are of the religious problem in the future, the greater the danger of our putting the divine germ within us to some ridiculous or demoniacal use, puffing ourselves up with it instead of remaining conscious that we are no more than the stable in which the Lord is born. (53)

What is needed are a few illuminating truths, but not articles of faith. Where an intelligible truth works, it finds in faith a willing ally; for faith has always helped when thinking and understanding could not quite make the grade. Understanding is never the handmaiden of faith—on the contrary, faith completes understanding. To educate men to a faith they do not understand is certainly a well-meant undertaking, but one runs the risk of creating an attitude that believes everything it does not understand. (53)

Theology does not help people who are looking for the key, because theology demands faith, and faith cannot be made. It is in the truest sense a gift of grace. We moderns are faced with the necessity of rediscovering the life of the spirit; we must experience it anew for ourselves. It is the only way in which to break the spell that binds us to the cycle of biological events. (30)

So long as religion is only faith and outward form, and the religious function is not experienced in our own souls, nothing of any importance has happened. It has yet to be understood that the *mysterium magnum* is not only an actuality but is first and foremost rooted in the human psyche. The man who does not know this from his own experience may be a most learned theologian, but he has no idea of religion and still less of education. (58)

Belief is no adequate substitute for inner experience, and where this is absent, even a strong faith which came miraculously as a gift of grace may depart equally miraculously. People call faith the true religious experience, but they do not stop to consider that actually it is a secondary phenomenon arising from the fact that something happened to us in the first place which instilled *pistis* into us—that is, trust and loyalty. (82)

Religious experience is absolute; it cannot be disputed. You can only say that you have never had such an experience, whereas your opponent will reply: "Sorry, I have." And there your discussion will come to an end. (60)

The primitive mentality did not *invent* myths, it *experienced* them. Myths are original revelations of the preconscious psyche, involuntary statements about unconscious psychic happenings, and anything but allegories of physical processes.

Such allegories would be an idle amusement for an unscientific intellect. Myths, on the contrary, have a vital meaning. Not merely do they represent, they *are* the mental life of the primitive tribe, which immediately falls to pieces and decays when it loses its mythological heritage, like a man who has lost his soul. A tribe's mythology is its living religion, whose loss is always and everywhere, even among the civilized, a moral catastrophe. But religion is a vital link with psychic process independent of and beyond consciousness, in the dark hinterland of the psyche. (62)

Religious sentimentality instead of the *numinosum* of divine experience: this is the well-known characteristic of a religion that has lost its living mystery. It is readily understandable that such a religion is incapable of giving help or having any other moral effect. (60)

I am convinced that the growing impoverishment of symbols has a meaning. It is a development that has an inner consistency. Everything that we have not thought about, and that has therefore been deprived of a meaningful connection with our developing consciousness, has got lost. If we now try to cover our nakedness with the gorgeous trappings of the East, as the theosophists do, we would be playing our own history false. A man does not sink down to beggary only to pose afterwards as an Indian potentate.

It seems to me that it would be far better stoutly to avow our spiritual poverty, our symbol-lessness, instead of feigning a legacy to which we are not the legitimate heirs at all. We are, surely, the rightful heirs of Christian symbolism, but somehow we have squandered this heritage. We have let the house our fathers built fall into decay, and now we try to break into Oriental palaces that our fathers never knew. (19)

The history of Protestantism has been one of chronic iconoclasm. One wall fell after another. And the work of destruction was not too difficult once the authority of the

Church had been shattered. We all know how, in large things as in small, in general as well as in particular, piece after piece collapsed, and how the alarming poverty of symbols that is now the condition of our life came about.

With that, the power of the Church has vanished too—a fortress robbed of its bastions and casemates, a house whose walls have been plucked away, exposed to all the winds of the world and its dangers. Although this is, properly speaking, a lamentable collapse that offends our sense of history, the disintegration of Protestantism into nearly four hundred denominations is yet a sure sign that the restlessness continues.

The Protestant is cast out into a state of defenselessness that might well make the natural man shudder. His enlightened consciousness, of course, refuses to take cognizance of this fact, and is quietly looking elsewhere for what has been lost to Europe. We seek the effective images, the thought-forms that satisfy the restlessness of heart and mind, and we find the treasures of the East. (19)

At a time when a large part of mankind is beginning to discard Christianity, it may be worth our while to try to understand why it was accepted in the first place. It was accepted as a means of escape from the brutality and unconsciousness of the ancient world. As soon as we discard it, the old brutality returns in force, as has been made overwhelmingly clear by contemporary events. . . .

We have had bitter experience of what happens when a whole nation finds the moral mask too stupid to keep up. The beast breaks loose, and a frenzy of demoralization sweeps over the civilized world. (78)

Christian education has done all that is humanly possible; but it has not been enough. Too few people have experienced the divine image as the innermost possession of their own souls. (58)

Religious symbols are phenomena of life, plain facts and not intellectual opinions. If the Church clung for so long to the idea that the sun rotates around the earth, and then abandoned this contention in the nineteenth century, she can always appeal to the psychological truth that for millions of people, the sun did revolve round the earth and that it was only in the nineteenth century that any major portion of mankind became sufficiently sure of the intellectual function to grasp the proof of the earth's planetary nature. Unfortunately, there is no "truth" unless there are people to understand it. (58)

Between the religion of a people and its actual mode of life there is always a compensatory relation, otherwise religion would have no practical significance at all. Beginning with the highly moral religion of the Persians and the notorious dubiousness—even in antiquity—of Persian habits of life, right down to our "Christian" epoch, when the religion of love assisted in the greatest blood-bath in the world's history—wherever we turn this rule holds. (56)

To the degree that the modern man is passionately concerned with anything and everything rather than religion and its prime object—original sin—[they] have mostly vanished into the unconscious. That is why, today, nobody believes in either. People accuse psychology of dealing in squalid fantasies, and yet even a cursory glance at ancient religions and the history of morals should be sufficient to convince them of the demons hidden in the human soul.

This disbelief goes hand in hand with a blank incomprehension of religion and its meaning. (78)

The great events of our world as planned and executed by man do not breathe the spirit of Christianity but rather of unadorned paganism. These things originate in a psychic condition that has remained archaic and has not even been remotely touched by Christianity.

The Church assumes, not altogether without reason, that the fact of *semel credidose* (having once believed) leaves certain traces behind it; but of these traces nothing is to be seen in the broad march of events. Christian civilization has proved hollow to a terrifying degree; it is all veneer, but the inner man has remained untouched and therefore unchanged. His soul is out of key with his external beliefs; in his soul, the Christian has not kept pace with his external developments. Yes, everything is to be found outside—in image and in word, in Church and Bible—but never inside. Inside reign the archaic gods, supreme as of old. (58)

All of us who have had a religious education are deeply impressed by the idea that Christianity entered into history without an historical past, like a stroke of lightning out of a clear sky. This attitude was necessary, but I am convinced that it is not true. Everything has its history, everything has "grown," and Christianity, which is supposed to have appeared suddenly as a unique revelation from heaven, undoubtedly also has its history.

Moreover, how it began is as clear as daylight. I need not speak of the priests' clothing, which is borrowed from pagan times, for the fundamental ideas of the Christian Church also have their predecessors. But a break in continuity has occurred because of the uniqueness of Christianity. It is exactly as if we had built a cathedral over a pagan temple and no longer knew that it is still there underneath.

The result is that the inner correspondence with the outer God-image is undeveloped through lack of psychic culture and has remained stuck in paganism. (20)

The fact is that the archetypal images are so packed with meaning in themselves that people never think of asking what they really do mean. That the gods die from time to time is due to man's sudden discovery that they do not mean anything, that they are made by human hands, useless idols of wood and stone. In reality, however, he has merely discovered that up till then he has never thought about his images at all. (19)

For thousands of years, the mind of man has worried about the sick soul, perhaps even earlier than it did about the sick body. The propitiation of gods, the perils of the soul and its salvation, these are not yesterday's problems. Religions are psychotherapeutic systems in the truest sense of the word, and on the grandest level. They express the whole range of the psychic problem in mighty images; they are the avowal and recognition of the soul, and at the same time, the revelation of the soul's nature. From this universal foundation, no human soul is cut off; only the individual consciousness that has lost its connection with the psychic totality remains caught in the illusion that the soul is a small circumscribed area, a fit subject for "scientific" theorizing. The loss of this great relationship is the prime evil of neurosis. (75)

The ways and customs of childhood, once so sublimely good, can hardly be laid aside even when their harmfulness has long since been proved. The same, only on a gigantic scale, is true of historical changes of attitude. A collective attitude is equivalent to a religion, and changes of religion constitute one of the most painful chapters in the world's history. In this respect, our age is afflicted with a blindness that has no parallel.

We think we have only to declare an accepted article of faith incorrect and invalid, and we shall be psychologically rid of all the traditional effects of Christianity or Judaism. We believe in enlightenment, as if an intellectual change of front somehow had a profounder influence on the emotional processes or even on the unconscious. We entirely forget that the religion of the last two thousand years is a psychological attitude, a definite form and manner or adaptation to the world without and within, that lays down a definite cultural pattern and creates an atmosphere, which remains wholly uninfluenced by any intellectual denials. (56)

You are sure to know the home-truth that prayer is not only of great importance, but has also a great effect upon human psychology. If you take the concept of prayer in its widest sense and if you include also Buddhist contemplation and Hindu meditation (as being equivalent to prayer), one can say that it is the most universal form of religious or philosophical concentration of the mind, and thus not only one of the most original but also the most frequent means to change the conditions of the mind.

If this psychological method had been inefficient, it would have been extinguished long ago, but nobody with a certain amount of human experience could deny its efficacy. (3)

Fanaticism is always a sign of repressed doubt. You can study that in the history of the Church. Always in those times when the Church begins to waver the style becomes fanatical, or fanatical sects spring up, because the secret doubt has to be quenched. When one is really convinced, one is perfectly calm and can discuss one's belief as a personal point of view without any particular resentment. (5)

Introversion is, if one may express it, the "style" of the East, an habitual and collective attitude, just as extraversion is the "style" of the West. Introversion is felt here as something abnormal, morbid, or otherwise objectionable. . . . In the East, however, our cherished extraversion is depreciated as illusory desirousness. (28)

We Westerners knew only how to tame and subdue the psyche; we knew nothing about its methodical development and its functions. Our civilization is still young, and young civilizations need all the arts of the animal-tamer to make the defiant barbarian and the savage in us more-or-less tractable. But at a higher cultural level, we must forgo compulsion and turn to self-development. (51)

Just as the unconscious world of mythological images speaks indirectly, through the experience of external things, to [one] who surrenders himself wholly to the outer world, so the real world and its demands find their way indirectly to the individual who has surrendered himself wholly to the soul; for no [one] can escape both realities. If he is intent only on outer reality, he must live his myth; if he is turned only toward the inner reality, he must dream his outer, so-called real life. (56)

We Europeans are not the only people on the earth. We are just a peninsula of Asia, and on that continent there are old civilizations where people have trained their minds in introspective psychology for thousands of years, whereas we began with our psychology not even yesterday but only this morning. (5)

What are religions? Religions are psychotherapeutic systems. What are we doing, we psychotherapists? We are trying to heal the suffering of the human mind, of the human psyche or the human soul, and religions deal with the same problem. (5)

The extraverted tendency of the West and the introverted tendency of the East have one important purpose in common: both make desperate efforts to conquer the mere naturalness of life. It is the assertion of mind over matter—a symptom of the youthfulness of man, still delighting in the use of the most powerful weapon ever devised by nature: the conscious mind. The afternoon of humanity, in a distant future, may yet evolve a different ideal. In time, even conquest will cease to be the dream. (28)

The mere act of enlightenment may have destroyed the spirits of nature, but not the psychic factors that correspond to them, such as suggestibility, lack of criticism, fearfulness, propensity to superstition and prejudice—in short, all those qualities which make [demonic-like] possession possible.

Even though nature is de-psychized, the psychic conditions which breed demons are as actively at work as ever. The demons have not really disappeared, but have merely taken on another form: they have become unconsciously psychic forces. (12)

By an inevitable decree of fate, the West is becoming acquainted with the peculiar facts of Eastern spirituality. It is useless to belittle these facts, or to build false and treacherous bridges over yawning gaps. Instead of learning the spiritual techniques of the East by heart and imitating them in a thoroughly [Western] way, it would be far more to the point to find out whether there exists in the unconscious an introverted tendency similar to that which has become the guiding spiritual principle of the East. We should then be in a position to build on our own ground with our own methods. If we snatch these things directly from the East, we have merely indulged our Western acquisitiveness. (28)

In each of these mythological images, there is a little piece of human psychology and human fate, a remnant of the joys and sorrows that have repeated countless times in our ancestral history, and on the average, follow ever the same course. It is like a deeply graven riverbed in the psyche, in which the waters of life, instead of flowing along as before in a broad but shallow stream, suddenly swell into a mighty river.

So it is not surprising that when an archetypal situation occurs, we suddenly feel an extraordinary sense of release, as though transported, or caught by an overwhelming power. At such moments, we are no longer individuals, but the race: the voice of all humanity resounds in us. (46)

# OUR DIVINE SOUL: THE FONT OF MYSTICISM AND THE PARANORMAL

If we consider the psyche as a whole, we come to the conclusion that the unconscious psyche likewise exists in a space-time continuum where time is no longer time and space no longer space. Accordingly, causality ceases too. Physics has reached the same frontier. (3)

In religious matters, it is a well-known fact that we cannot understand a thing until we have experienced it inwardly. (3)

Were it not a fact of experience that supreme values reside in the soul ... psychology would not interest me in the least, for the soul would then be nothing but a miserable vapor. I know, however, from hundredfold experience that it is nothing of the sort, but on the contrary contains the equivalents of everything that has been formulated in dogma and a good deal more, which is just what enables it to be an eye destined to behold the light. This requires limitless range, and unfathomable depth of vision. I have been accused of "deifying the soul." Not I but God himself has deified it! (58)

It is only through the psyche that we can establish that God acts upon us, but we are unable to distinguish whether these actions emanate from God or from the unconscious. . . . Strictly speaking, the God-image does not coincide with the unconscious as such, but with a special content of it, namely the archetype of the self. It is this archetype from which we can no longer distinguish the God-image empirically.

We can arbitrarily postulate a difference between these two entities, but that does not help us at all. On the contrary, it only helps us to separate man from God, and prevents God from becoming man. Faith is certainly right when it impresses on man's mind and heart how infinitely far away and inaccessible God is; but it also teaches his nearness, his immediate presence, and it is just this nearness which has to be empirically real if it is not to lose all significance.

Only that which acts upon me do I recognize as real and actual. But that which does not act upon me might as well not exist. The religious need longs for wholeness, and therefore lays hold of the images of wholeness offered by the unconscious, which, independently of our conscious mind, rise up from the depths of our psychic nature. (17)

Only the mystics bring creativity into religion. (41)

Just as, in its lower reaches, the psyche loses itself in the organic-material substrate, so in its upper reaches it resolves itself into a "spiritual" form about which we know as little as we do about the functional basis of instinct. (44)

We have stripped all things of their mystery and numinosity: nothing is holy any longer. (4)

*I* did not attribute a religious function to the soul, I merely produced the facts which prove the soul . . . possesses a religious attitude. I did not invent or insinuate this function, it produces itself of its own accord without being prompted thereto by any opinions or suggestions of mine.

With a truly tragic delusion, theologians fail to see that it is not a matter of proving the existence of light, but of blind people who do not know that their eyes could see. It is high time we realized that it is pointless to praise the light and preach it if nobody can see it. It is much more needful to teach people the art of seeing.

For it is obvious that far too many people are incapable of establishing a connection between the sacred figures and their own psyche: they cannot see to what extent the equivalent images are lying dormant in their own unconscious. In order to facilitate this inner vision, we must first clear the way for the faculty of seeing. How this is to be done without psychology, that is, without making contact with the psyche, is frankly, beyond my comprehension. (58)

To have soul is the whole venture of life, for soul is a life-giving daemon who plays his elfin game above and below human existence, for which reason—in the realm of dogma—he is threatened and propitiated with superhuman punishments and blessings that go far beyond the possible deserts of human beings. Heaven and hell are the fates meted out to the soul and not to civilized man, who in his nakedness and timidity would have no idea of what to do with himself in a heavenly Jerusalem. (19)

Whoever speaks of the reality of the soul or psyche is accused of "psychologism." Psychology is spoken of as if it were "only" psychology and nothing else. The notion that there can be psychic factors which correspond to the divine figures is regarded as a devaluation of the latter. It smacks of blasphemy to think that a religious experience is a psychic process; for, so it is argued, a religious experience "is not *only* psychological." Anything psychic is only Nature and therefore, people think, nothing religious can come out of it.

At the same time, such critics never hesitate to derive all religions—with the exception of their own—from the nature of the psyche. (58)

For thousands of years, rites of initiation have been teaching rebirth from the spirit; yet, strangely enough, man forgets again and again the meaning of divine procreation. Though this may be poor testimony to the strength of the spirit, the penalty for misunderstanding is neurotic decay, embitterment, atrophy, and sterility. It is easy enough to drive the spirit out of the door, but when we have done so the meal has lost its savour—the salt of the earth.

Fortunately, we have proof that the spirit always renews its strength in the fact that the essential teaching of the initiations is handed on from generation to generation. Ever and again, there are human beings who understand what it means that God is their father. The equal balance of the flesh and the spirit is not lost to the world. (17)

Agnosticism maintains that it does not possess any knowledge of God or anything metaphysical, overlooking the fact that one never *possesses* a metaphysical belief but is *possessed* by it. (17)

"God" is a primordial experience of man, and from the remotest times humanity has taken inconceivable pains either to portray this baffling experience, to assimilate it by means of interpretation, speculation, and dogma, or else to deny it. And again and again it has happened, and still happens, that one hears too much about the "good" God and knows him too well, so that one confuses him with one's own ideas and regards them as sacred because they can be traced back a couple of thousand years. This is a superstition and an idolatry every bit as bad as the Bolshevik delusion that "God" can be educated out of existence. (22)

But God himself cannot flourish if man's soul is starved. (86)

It is not ethical principles, however lofty, or creeds, however orthodox, that lay the foundations for the freedom and autonomy of the individual, but simply and solely the empirical awareness, the incontrovertible experience of an intensely personal, reciprocal relationship between man and an extramundane authority which acts as a counterpoise to the "world" and its "reason." (82)

It would be a regrettable mistake if anybody should take my observations as a kind of proof of the existence of God. They only prove the existence of an archetypal God-image, which to my mind is the most we can assert about God psychologically. (60)

The competence of psychology as an empirical science only goes so far as to establish on the basis of comparative research, whether for instance the imprint found in the psyche can or cannot reasonably be termed a "God-image." Nothing positive or negative has thereby been asserted about the possible existence of God, any more than the archetype of the "hero" proves the actual existence of a hero. (58)

The idea of the moral order and of God belong to the ineradicable substrate of the human soul. That is why any honest psychology, which is not blinded by the garish conceits of enlightenment, must come to terms with these facts. They cannot be explained away and killed with irony.

In analysis, we can do without a God-image, but in psychology, it is a definite fact that has got to be reckoned with, just as we have to reckon with "affect," "instinct," and "mother." (31)

The idea of God is an absolutely necessary psychological function of an irrational nature, which has nothing whatever to do with the question of God's existence. The human intellect can never answer this question, still less give any proof of God. Moreover, such proof is superfluous, for the idea of an all-powerful divine Being is present everywhere, unconsciously if not consciously, because it is an archetype. (81)

I have been asked so often whether I believe in the existence of God that I am somewhat concerned lest I be taken for an adherent of "psychologism" far more commonly than I suspect. What most people overlook or seem unable to understand is the fact that I regard the psyche as real. They believe only in physical facts, and must consequently come to the conclusion that either the uranium itself or the laboratory equipment created the atom bomb. That is no less absurd than the assumption that a non-real psyche is responsible for it. God is an obvious psychic and non-physical fact: that is, a fact that can be established psychically but not physically. (17)

The materialistic error was probably unavoidable at first. Since the throne of God could not be discovered among the galactic systems, the inference was that God had never existed. The second unavoidable error is psychologism; if God is anything, he must be an illusion derived from certain motives—from will to power, for instance, or from repressed sexuality.

These arguments are not new. Much the same thing was said by the Christian missionaries who overthrow the idols of heathen gods. But whereas the early missionaries were conscious of serving a new God by combating the old ones, modern iconoclasts are unconscious of the one in whose names they are destroying old values. (60)

Buddha was once asked by one of his disciples why all his disciples, though redeemed, didn't possess the wonderful gifts of the fourth degree of contemplation: namely, sitting on the air, walking through walls, remembering their past lives, seeing things in the future, and touching the sun and moon. Buddha quietly turned the disciple's mind to the path of redemption and let him see how foolish it was to ask for such miracles. That is what the superior Indian thinks about the claims of the yogins. (3)

Parapsychology plays a subtle part in psychology because it lurks everywhere behind the surface of things. But, as the facts are difficult to catch, their theoretical aspect is still more elusive on account of its transcendent character. When certain people hold that it is something like a fourth dimension, they don't seem to be very far off the truth. (3)

In as much as any function of consciousness can be directed, controlled and differentiated, intuition can also be practiced and differentiated. That you can perceive things which your senses would not allow you to catch hold of, or your thinking would not allow you to infer, forms an additional problem. It forces us to speculate about the nature of time and space. The fact that extra-sensory perception is real proves that time and space are psychically relative. That means that they can be more-or-less annihilated. If that is the case, an extreme is also possible where time and space don't exist at all. (3)

If there were to be a conscious existence after death, it would, so it would seem to me, have to continue on the level of consciousness attained by humanity, which in any age has an upper though variable limit. There are many human beings who throughout their lives and at the moment of death lag behind their own potentialities and—even more important—behind the knowledge which has been brought to consciousness by other human beings during their own lifetimes. Hence their demand to attain in death that share of awareness which they failed to win in life. (6)

Death is indeed a fearful piece of brutality; there is no sense in pretending otherwise. It is brutal not only as a physical event, but far more so psychically: a human being is torn away from us, and what remains is the icy stillness of death. There no longer exists any hope of a relationship, for all the bridges have been smashed at one blow. Those who deserve a long life are cut off in the prime of their years, and good-for-nothings live to a ripe old age. This is a cruel reality which we have no right to sidestep. The actual experience of the cruelty and wantonness of death can so embitter us that we conclude there is no merciful God, no justice, and no kindness.

From another point of view, however, death appears as a joyful event. In the light of eternity, it is a wedding, a *mysterium coniunctionis.* The soul attains, as it were, its missing half, it achieves wholeness. On Greek sarcophagi the joyous element was represented by dancing girls, on Etruscan tombs by banquets. When the pious Cabbalist Rabbi Simon ben Jochai came to die, his friends said that he was celebrating his wedding. To this day it is the custom in many regions to hold a picnic on the graves of All Soul's Day. Such customs express the feeling that death is really a festive occasion. (6)

The decisive question for man is: Is he related to something infinite or not? That is the telling question of his life. Only if we know that the thing which truly matters is the infinite can we avoid fixing our interest upon futilities, and upon all kinds of goals which are not of real importance. Thus we demand that the world grant us recognition for qualities which we regard as personal possessions: our talent or our beauty.

The more a man lays stress on false possessions, and the less sensitivity he has for what is essential, the less satisfying is his life. He feels limited because he has limited aims, and the result is envy and jealousy. If we understand and feel that here in this life we already have a link with the infinite, desires and attitudes change. In the final analysis, we count for something only because of the essential we embody, and if we do not embody that, life is wasted. In our relationships to other men, too, the crucial question is whether an element of boundlessness is expressed in the relationship. (6)

It is only through the psyche that we can establish that God acts upon us, but we are unable to distinguish whether these actions emanate from God or from the unconscious. We cannot tell whether God and the unconscious are two different entities. Both are borderline concepts for transcendental contents. But empirically, it can be established, with a sufficient degree of probability, that there is in the unconscious an archetype of wholeness which manifests itself spontaneously in dreams, and a tendency, independent of the conscious will, to relate other archetypes to this center. Consequently, it does not seem improbable that the archetype produces a symbolism which has always characterized and expressed the Deity. . . . The God-image does not coincide with the unconscious as such, but with a special content of it: namely, the archetype of the self. It is this archetype from which we can no longer distinguish the God-image empirically. (6)

Synchronicity is no more baffling or mysterious than the discontinuities of physics. It is only the ingrained belief in the sovereign power of causality that creates intellectual difficulties and makes it appear unthinkable that causeless events exist or could ever occur. . . . Meaningful coincidences are thinkable as pure chance. But the more they multiply and the greater and more exact the correspondence is, the more their probability sinks and their unthinkability increases, until they can no longer be regarded as pure chance but, for lack of a causal explanation, have to be thought of as meaningful arrangements. . . . Their "inexplicability" is not due to the fact that the cause is unknown, but to the fact that a cause is not even thinkable in intellectual terms. (6)

It would be blasphemy to assert that God can manifest Himself everywhere save only in the human soul. Indeed the very intimacy of the relationship between God and the soul automatically precludes any devaluation of the latter. It would be going perhaps too far to speak of an affinity. But at all events, the soul must contain in itself the faculty of relation to God: that is, a correspondence; otherwise, a connection could never come about. This correspondence is, in psychological terms, the archetype of the God-image. (6)

My preoccupation with the psychology of unconscious processes long ago compelled me to look about for another principle of explanation, because the causality principle seemed to me inadequate to explain certain remarkable phenomena of the psychology of the unconscious. Thus I found that there are psychic parallelisms which cannot be related through another principle: namely, the contingency of events. This connection of events seemed to me essentially given by the fact of their relative simultaneity, hence the term "synchronistic."

It seems, indeed, as though time, far from being an abstraction, is a concrete continuum which contains qualities or basic conditions that manifest themselves simultaneously in different places through parallelisms that cannot be explained causally, as for example, in cases of the simultaneous occurrence of identical thoughts, symbols, or psychic states. (6)

God is not a *statistical* truth, hence it is just as stupid to try to prove the existence of God as to deny him. If a person feels happy, he needs neither proof nor counterproof. Also, there is no reason to suppose that "happiness" or "sadness" cannot be experienced. God is a universal experience which is obfuscated only by silly rationalism and an equally silly theology. (3)

No one can know what the ultimate things are. We must therefore take them as we experience them. And if such experience helps to make life healthier, more beautiful, more complete, and more satisfactory to yourself and to those you love, you may safely say: "This was the grace of God."

No transcendental truth is thereby demonstrated, and we must confess in all humility that religious experience is *extra ecclesiam*, subjective, and liable to boundless error. (60)

Your sympathy over the death of my last close friend, Albert Oeri, was veritable balm. One can indeed feel the pain of such a loss without making oneself guilty of undue sentimentality. One notices on all such occasions how age gradually pushes one out of time and the world into wider and uninhabited spaces where one feels at first rather lonely and strange.

You have written so sympathetically and perceptively in our book of the peculiarities of old age that you will have an understanding heart for this mood. The imminence of death and the vision of the world in *conspectu mortis* is in truth a curious experience: the sense of the present stretches out beyond today, looking back into centuries gone by, and forward into futures yet unborn. (3)

This spectacle of old age would be unendurable did we not know that our psyche reaches into a region held captive neither by change in time nor by limitations of place. In that form of being, our birth is a death and our death a birth. The scales of the whole hang balanced. (3)

You ask me in your letter about the spook phenomena. Well, this is a point where I have to give up. I cannot explain the locally-bound spook phenomena. There is a factor in it that is just not psychological. We have to look elsewhere for a proper explanation. I'm inclined to believe that something of the human soul remains after death, since already in this conscious life we have evidence that the psyche exists in a relative space and in a relative time, that is in a relatively non-extended and eternal state. Possibly the spook phenomena are indications of such existences. (3)

As in the psychic world, there are no bodies moving through space, there is also no time. The archetypal world is "eternal," that is, outside time, and it is everywhere, as there is no space under psychic, that is, archetypal conditions. Where an archetype prevails, we can expect synchronistic phenomena, that is, acausal correspondences, which consist in a parallel arrangement of facts in time. The arrangement is not the effect of a cause. It just happens, being a consequence of the fact that causality is merely a statistical truth. (3)

Far from being a material world, this is a psychic world, which allows us to make only indirect and hypothetical inferences about the real nature of matter. The psychic alone has immediate reality, and this includes all forms of the psychic, even "unreal" ideas and thoughts which refer to nothing "external." We may call them "imagination" or "delusion," but that does not detract in any way from their effectiveness. Indeed, there is no "real" thought that cannot, at times, be thrust aside by an "unreal" one, thus proving that the latter is stronger and more effective than the former.

Greater than all physical dangers are the tremendous effects of delusional ideas, which are yet denied all reality by our world-blinded consciousness. Our much-vaunted reason and our boundlessly overestimated will are sometimes utterly powerless in the face of "unreal" thoughts. The world powers that rule over all humanity, for good or ill, are unconscious psychic factors, and it is they that bring unconsciousness into being and hence create the *sine qua non* for the existence of any world at all. We are steeped in a world that was created by our own psyche. (67)

Everybody is free to believe anything which seems to fit about things of which we know nothing. Nobody knows whether there is reincarnation, and equally one does not know that there is none. Buddha himself was convinced of reincarnation, but he himself on being asked twice by his disciples about it, left it quite open whether there is continuity of personality or not. Certainly we do not know where we come from, nor where we are going, or why we are here at the present time. I think it is right to believe that having done the best we could do here, we are also best prepared for things to come. (3)

If the human [soul] is anything, it must be of unimaginable complexity and diversity, so that it cannot possibly be approached through a mere psychology of instinct. I can only gaze with wonder and awe at the depths and heights of our psychic nature. Its non-spatial universe conceals an untold abundance of images which have accumulated over millions of years of living development and become fixed in the organism.

My consciousness is like an eye that penetrates to the

most distant spaces, yet it is the psychic non-ego that fills them with non-spatial images. And these images are not pale shadows, but tremendously powerful psychic factors. . . . Beside this picture I would like to place the spectacle of the starry heavens at night, for the only equivalent of the universe within is the universe without; and just as I reach this world through the medium of the body, so I reach that world through the medium of the psyche. (3)

The idea that mescaline could produce a *transcendental* experience is shocking. The drug merely uncovers the normally unconscious functional layer of perceptional and emotional variants, which are only psychologically transcendent but by no means "transcendental," that is, metaphysical.

Such an experiment may be in practice good for people having a desire to convince themselves of the real existence of an unconscious psyche. It could give them a fair idea of its reality. But I could never accept mescaline as a means to convince people of the possibility of spiritual experience over against their materialism. It is, on the contrary, an excellent demonstration of Marxist materialism: mescaline is the drug by which you can manipulate the brain so that it produces even so-called "spiritual" experiences. That is the ideal case for Bolshevism and its "brave new world." (3)

People who think they know the reasons for everything are unaware of the obvious fact that the existence of the universe itself is one big unfathomable secret, and so is our human existence. You can be glad to have such a conviction [that God exists], like a man who is in a happy frame of mind, even if nobody else, not even himself, knows why. But certainly nobody could prove to him that he is unhappy, or that his feeling happy is an illusion. (3)

The only scientific approach to the question of survival [after bodily death] is the recognition of the fact that the psyche is capable of extrasensory perception, namely of telepathy and of precognition, particularly the latter. This fact proves a relative independence of the psyche from time and space. This means that the two elements of time and space, indispensable for change, are relatively without importance for the psyche.

In other words, the psyche is up to a certain point not subject to corruptibility. That's all we know. Of course, one can have experiences of a very convincing subjective nature which need no support through scientific possibilities. But for those people not possessing the gift of belief, it may be helpful to remember that science itself points to the possibility of survival. (3)

Astrology is one of the intuitive methods like the *I Ching*, geomantics, and other divinatory procedures. It is based upon the synchronicity principle: that is, meaningful coincidence. I have explored experimentally three intuitive methods: the *I Ching*, geomantics, and astrology.

Astrology is a naively projected psychology in which the different attitudes and temperaments of man are represented as gods and identified with planets and zodiacal constellations. While studying astrology I have applied it to concrete cases many times. . . .

There is no psychological exposition of astrology yet, on account of the fact that the empirical foundation in the sense of a science has not yet been laid. The reason for this is that astrology does not follow the principle of causality, but depends, like all intuitive methods, on acausality. Undoubtedly, astrology today is flourishing as never before in the past, but it is still most unsatisfactorily explored despite very frequent use. It is an apt tool only when used intelligently. It is not at all foolproof and when used by a rationalistic and narrow mind, it is a definite nuisance. (3)

Since you want to know my opinion about astrology, I can tell you that I've been interested in this particular activity of the human psyche for more than 30 years. As I am a psychologist, I'm chiefly interested in the particular light the horoscope sheds on certain complications in the character. In cases of difficult psychological diagnosis, I usually get a horoscope in order to have a further point of view from an entirely different angle. I must say that I very often found that the astrological data elucidated certain points which I otherwise would have been unable to understand.

From such experiences, I formed the opinion that astrology is of particular interest to the psychologist, since it contains a sort of psychological experience which we call "projected." This means that we find the psychological facts, as it were, in the constellations. This originally gave rise to the ideas that these factors derive from the stars, whereas they are merely in a relation of synchronicity with them.

I admit that this is a very curious fact which throws a peculiar light on the structure of the human mind. What I miss in astrological literature is chiefly the statistical method by which certain fundamental facts could be scientifically established. (3)

It remained for modern science to despiritualize Nature through its so-called objective knowledge of matter. All anthropomorphic projections were withdrawn from the object one after another, with a twofold result: firstly, man's mystical identity with nature was curtailed as never before, and secondly, the projections falling back into the human soul caused such a terrific activation of the unconscious that in modern times man was compelled to postulate the existence of an unconscious psyche. Instead of the lost Olympian gods, there was disclosed the inner wealth of the soul which lies in every man's heart. (80)

Nobody can say where man ends. That is the beauty of it. The unconscious of man can reach God knows where. There we are going to make discoveries. (1)

There is no other way open to us. We are forced to resort to conscious decisions and solutions where formerly we trusted ourselves to natural happenings. Every problem, therefore, brings the possibility of a widening of consciousness, but also the necessity of saying goodbye to childlike unconsciousness and trust in nature.

This necessity is a psychic fact of such importance that it constitutes one of the most essential symbolic teachings of the Christian religion. It is the sacrifice of the merely natural man, of the unconscious, ingenuous being whose tragic career began with the eating of the apple in Paradise. The biblical fall of man presents the dawn of consciousness as a curse. And as a matter of fact, it is in this light that we first look upon every problem that forces us to greater consciousness and separates us even further from the paradise of unconscious childhood. (74)

If we were conscious of the spirit of the age, we should know why we are so inclined to account for everything on physical grounds: we should know that it is because, up till now, too much was accounted for in terms of spirit. This realization would at once make us critical of our bias. We would say: most likely we are now making exactly the same mistake on the other side.

We delude ourselves with the thought that we know much more about matter than about a "metaphysical" mind or spirit, and so we over-estimate material causation and believe that it alone affords us a true explanation of life. But matter is just as inscrutable as mind. As to the ultimate things, we can know nothing, and only when we admit this do we return to a state of equilibrium. (21)

Western consciousness is by no means the only kind of consciousness there is: it is historically conditioned and geographically limited, and representative of only part of humanity. The widening of our consciousness ought not to proceed at the expense of other kinds of consciousness. It should come about through the development of those elements of our psyche which are analogous to those of the alien psyche, just as the East cannot do without our technology, science, and industry. The European invasion of the East was an act of violence on a grand scale, and it has left us with the duty—*noblesse oblige*—of understanding the mind of the East. This is perhaps more necessary than we realize at present. (84)

In general, meditation and contemplation have a bad reputation in the West. They are regarded as a particularly reprehensible form of idleness or as pathological narcissism. No one has time for self-knowledge or believes that it could serve any sensible purpose. Also, one knows in advance that it is not worth the trouble to know oneself, for any fool can know what he is.

We believe exclusively in doing and do not ask about the doer, who is judged only by achievements that have collective value. The general public seems to have taken cognizance of the existence of the unconscious psyche more than the so-called experts, but still nobody has drawn any conclusions from the fact that Western man confronts himself as a stranger and that self-knowledge is one of the most difficult and exacting of the arts. (41)

What if there were a living agency beyond our everyday human world—something even more purposeful than electrons? Do we delude ourselves in thinking that we possess and control our own psyches, and is what science calls the "psyche" not just a question-mark arbitrarily confined within the skull, but rather a door that opens upon the human world from a world beyond, allowing unknown and mysterious powers to act upon man and carry him on the wings of the night to a more than personal destiny? (59)

Grounds for an unusually intense fear of death are nowadays not far to seek: they are obvious enough, the more so as all life that is senselessly wasted and misdirected means death too. This may account for the unnatural intensification of the fear of death in our time, when life has lost its deeper meaning for so many people, forcing them to exchange the life-preserving rhythm of the aeons for the dread ticking of the clock. (29)

Through scientific understanding, our world has become dehumanized. Man feels himself isolated in the cosmos. He is no longer involved in nature and has lost his emotional participation in natural events, which hitherto had a symbolic meaning for him. Thunder is no longer the voice of a god, nor is lightning his avenging missile. No river contains a spirit, no tree means a man's life, no snake is the embodiment of wisdom, and no mountain still harbors a great demon. Neither do things speak to him nor can he speak to things, like stones, springs, plants, and animals. He no longer has a bush-soul identifying him with a wild animal. His immediate communication with Nature is gone forever. (4)

Life is a touchstone for the spirit. Spirit that drags a man away from life, seeking fulfillment only in itself, is a false spirit—though the man too is to blame, since he can choose whether he will give himself up to this spirit or not. Life and spirit are two powers or necessities between which man is placed. Spirit gives meaning to his life, and the possibility of his greatest developments. But life is essential to spirit, since its truth is nothing if it cannot live. (73)

Tao can be anything. I use another word to designate it, but it is poor enough. I call it *synchronicity*. The Eastern mind, when it looks at an ensemble of facts, accepts that ensemble as it is, but the Western mind divides it into entities, small quantities. . . . Not so the Eastern mind; it is interested in being together.

It is like this: you are standing on the sea-shore and the waves wash up an old hat, an old box, a shoe, a dead fish, and there they lie on the shore. You say, "Chance, nonsense!" The Chinese mind asks: "What does it mean that these things are together?" The Chinese mind experiments with that *being together and coming together at the right moment.* (5)

Only an exceedingly naïve and unconscious person could imagine that he is in a position to avoid sin. Psychology can no longer afford childish illusions of this kind;

it must ensure the truth and declare that unconsciousness is not only no excuse but is actually one of the most heinous sins. Human law may exempt it from punishment, but Nature avenges herself more mercilessly, for it is nothing to her whether a man is conscious of his sin or not. (29)

What we need is the development of the inner spiritual man, the unique individual whose treasure is hidden on the one hand in the symbols of our mythological tradition, and on the other hand in man's unconscious psyche. It is tragic that science and its philosophy discourage the individual, and that theology resists every reasonable attempt to understand its symbols. (3)

# EDUCATION, SOCIAL CHANGE, AND WORLD IMPROVEMENT

Our age wants to experience the psyche for itself. It wants original experience and not assumptions, though it is willing to make use of all the existing assumptions as a means to this end, including those of the recognized religions and the authentic sciences. . . . There can be no doubt that from the beginning of the nineteenth century—ever since the time of the French Revolution, the psyche has moved more and more into the foreground of man's interest, and with a steadily increasing power of attraction. (90)

Along the great highways of the world, everything seems desolate and outworn. Instinctively, modern man leaves the trodden paths to explore the byways and lanes, just as the man of the Greco-Roman world cast off his defunct Olympian gods and turned to the mystery cults of Asia. Our instinct turns outward, and appropriates Eastern theosophy and magic; but it also turns inward, and leads us to contemplate the dark background of the psyche. It does this with the same skepticism and the same ruthlessness which impelled the Buddha to sweep aside his two million gods that he might attain the original experience which alone is convincing. (90)

Life on this earth is balanced between an equal amount of pleasure and misery, even when it is at its best, and that *real progress* is only the psychological adaptation to the various forms of individual misery. Misery is relative. When many people possess two cars, the man with only one car [feels] deprived of the goods of this world and therefore entitled to overthrow the social order. (3)

Since we cannot imagine—unless we have lost our critical faculties altogether—that mankind today has attained the highest possible degree of consciousness, there must be some potential unconscious psyche left over whose development would result in a further extension and a higher differentiation of consciousness. No one can say how great or small this "remnant" might be, for we have no means of measuring the possible range of conscious development, let alone the extent of the unconscious. (63)

Thus, the sickness of dissociation in our world is at the same time a process of recovery, or rather, the climax of a period of pregnancy which heralds the throes of birth. A time of dissociation such as prevailed during the Roman Empire is simultaneously an age of rebirth. Not without reason do we date our era from the Age of Augustus, for that epoch saw the birth of the symbolical figure of Christ, who was invoked by the early Christians as the Fish, the Ruler of the aeon of Pisces which had just begun. He became the ruling spirit of the next two thousand years.

Like the teacher of wisdom in Babylonian legend, Oannes, he rose up from the sea, from the primeval darkness, and brought a world-period to an end. It is true that he said, "I am come not to bring peace but a sword." But that which brings division ultimately creates union. Therefore his teaching was one of all-uniting love. (40)

As you know, the main endeavor of all totalitarian States is to undermine personal relationships through fear and mistrust, the result being an atomized mass in which the human psyche is completely stifled. Even the relation between parents and children, the closest and most natural of all, is torn asunder by the State. All big organizations that pursue exclusively materialistic aims are the pacemakers of mass-mindedness. (3)

I will try to be simple. A political situation is the manifestation of a parallel psychological problem in millions of individuals. This problem is largely unconscious, which makes it particularly dangerous. It consists of a conflict between a conscious (ethical, religious, philosophical, social, political, and psychological) standpoint and an unconscious one which is characterized by the same aspects but represented in a "lower," that is, more archaic form. So instead of a constructive use of political power with the aim of attaining an equilibrium of freely developing forces, a destructive tendency to extend suppression over the whole world through attaining mere superiority of power. Instead of psychology, use of psychological means to extinguish the individual spark and to inhibit the development of consciousness and intelligence. (3)

Technology and "social welfare" provide nothing to overcome our spiritual stagnation, and they give us no answer to our spiritual dissatisfaction and restlessness, on account of which we are threatened from within as from without. We have not understood yet that the discovery of the unconscious means an enormous spiritual task, which must be accomplished if we wish to preserve our civilization. (3)

❖     ❖     ❖

Whatever we fight about in the outside world is also a battle in our inner selves. For we must finally admit that humanity is not just an accumulation of individuals utterly different from one another, but possesses such a high degree of psychological collectivity that in comparison the individual appears merely as a slight variant. How shall we judge of this matter fairly if we cannot admit that it is also our own problem? Anyone who can admit this will first seek the solution in himself, and this in fact is the way all the great solutions begin. (85)

You are quite right when you say that the modern world prefers living *en masse* and thus forgets the bond with the past which is characteristic of every culture. The young people are not to blame, for it is quite understandable that they should keep an eye open for what is new and impressive about our so-called cultural achievements. But one must also realize that the real cultural good, the legacy of the past, is very often presented in such a boring and uninteresting way that it is almost a miracle if anyone can muster any enthusiasm for it. . . .

It seems to me perfectly possible to teach history in the widest sense not as dry-as-dust, lifeless book-knowledge but to understand it in terms of the fully alive present. All these things should be presented as coming out of our contemporary existence and not as dead relics of times outlived. This certainly faces the teacher with a hard and responsible task, but that's what a teacher is for.

A more than specialist education is always useful. I have never regretted knowing things outside my specialty. On the contrary, renewals never come from over-sophisticated specialized knowledge, but from a knowledge of subsidiary subjects which give us new points of view. A wider horizon benefits all of us and is also more natural to the human spirit than specialist knowledge that leads to a spiritual bottleneck. (3)

Your plan to establish prizes in the fields of human activity not yet covered by the Nobel Prize is indeed a very fine idea. Whereas the Nobel Prize only considers discoveries or merits concerning natural sciences and medicine (with the exception of the political "peace prize"), the psychic and spiritual welfare of man has been completely disregarded. Man's peace of mind, his mental balance and even his health largely depend upon mental and spiritual factors that cannot be substituted by physical conditions. If man's psychic health and happiness depended upon the proper food and other physical conditions of living, then all wealthy people should be healthy and happy, and all poor people mentally unbalanced, physically ill, and unhappy. But the contrary is true.

The great dangers threatening the life of millions are not physical factors, but mental folly and diabolical schemes causing mental epidemics in the mentally defenseless masses. There is no comparison between even the worst disasters or the greatest natural catastrophes (such as earthquakes, floods, and epidemics) and that which man can do to man today.

A prize should be given to people who successfully suppress the outpourings of political madness or of panic, or who produce great ideas enlarging the mental and spiritual horizon of man. (3)

I think we underrate in Europe the difficulties you have to put up with in America as soon as you try to communicate a certain humanistic education. I am afraid that your educational system produces the same technological and scientific one-sidedness and the same social welfare idealism as Russia. Most of your psychologists, as it seems to me, are still in the eighteenth century inasmuch as they believe that the human psyche is *tabula rasa* at birth, while all somewhat differentiated animals are born with specific instincts. [To them], man's psyche seems to be less [differentiated] than a weaver bird's or a bee's. (3)

Our whole society is split up by specialism, and the self-serving professions are so differentiated that none of them knows what the other is doing. There's nothing to be hoped for from the universities, since they turn out only specialists. Even psychology gives no thought to the unity of man, but has split into countless subdivisions, each with its own tests and specialist theories. Anyone who sought the wisdom that is needed would soon find himself in the situation of old Diogenes, who went looking for an [honest] man in the marketplace of Athens in broad daylight with a lantern in his hand. (3)

The coming new age will be as vastly different from ours as the world of the nineteenth century was from the twentieth, with its atomic physics and its psychology of the unconscious. Never before has mankind been torn into two halves, and never before was the power of absolute destruction given into the hand of man himself. (3)

Noise is certainly only one of the evils of our time, though perhaps the most obtrusive. The others are the gramophone, the radio, and now the blight of television. I was once asked by an organization of teachers why, in spite of the better food in elementary schools, the curriculum could no longer be completed nowadays.

The answer is: lack of concentration, too many distractions. Many children do their work to the accompaniment of the radio. So much is fed into them from outside that they no longer have to think of something they could do from inside themselves, which requires concentration. . . .

Noise is welcome because it drowns the inner instinctive warning. Fear seeks noisy company and pandemonium to scare away the demons; the primitive equivalents are yells, bullroarers, drums, fire-crackers, and bells. Noise, like crowds, gives a feeling of security; therefore, people love it and avoid doing anything about it as they instinctively feel the apotrapic magic it sends out. . . .

Noise protects us from painful reflection, it scatters our anxious dreams, it assures us that we are all in the same boat and creating such a racket that nobody will dare to attack us. Noise is so insistent, so overwhelmingly real, that everything else becomes a pale phantom. It relieves us of the effort to say or do anything, for the very air reverberates with the invincible power of our modernity.

The dark side of the picture is that we wouldn't have noise if we didn't secretly want it. Noise is not merely inconvenient or harmful, it is an unadmitted and uncomprehended means to an end: compensation of the fear which is only too well founded. If there were silence, their fear would make people reflect, and there's no telling what might then come to consciousness. Most people are afraid of silence. (3)

One of the most important points [about cultural differences] is one's attitude towards emotionality, and to what extent an affect is held to be controllable or not. The English believe in controlling emotions and bring up their children accordingly. Having emotions is "bad taste" and proof of "bad upbringing." The Italians cultivate their emotions and admire them, for which reason they become relatively harmless and at most absorb too much time and attention. The Germans feel entitled to their manly anger, the French adore analyzing their emotions rationally so as to not have to take them seriously. The Swiss, if they are well brought up, do not trust themselves to give vent to their emotions. The Indians, if influenced by Buddhism, habitually depotentiate their emotions by reciting a mantra.

Thus, in Ceylon, I once saw two peasants get their carts stuck together, which in any other part of the world would have led to endless vituperation. But they settled the matter by murmuring the mantra "aduca anatman" (passing disturbance—no soul). (3)

It is my conviction that the investigation of the psyche is the science of the future. Psychology is the youngest of the sciences and is only at the beginning of its development. It is, however, the science we need most. Indeed, it is becoming ever more obvious that it is not famine, not earthquakes, not microbes, not cancer, but man himself who is man's greatest danger to man, for the simple reason that there is no adequate protection against psychic epidemics, which are infinitely more devastating than the worst of natural catastrophes. The supreme danger which threatens individuals as well as whole nations is a *psychic danger.* (24)

The world today hangs by a thin thread, and that thread is the psyche of man. (1)

Why is it that we are especially interested in psychology just now? The answer is that everyone is in desperate need of it. Humanity seems to have reached a point where the concepts of the past are no longer adequate, and we begin to realize that our nearest and dearest are actually strangers to us, whose language we no longer understand.

It is beginning to dawn on us that the people living on the other side of the mountain are not made up exclusively of red-headed devils who are responsible for all the evil on this side of the mountain. A little of this uneasy suspicion has filtered through into the relations between the sexes: not everyone is utterly convinced that everything good is in "me" and everything evil is in "you."

Already we can find super-moderns who ask themselves in all seriousness whether there may not be something wrong with us, whether perhaps we are too unconscious, too antiquated, and whether this may not be the reason why, when confronted with difficulties in sexual relationships, we still continue to employ with disastrous results the methods of the Middle Ages, if not those of the caveman. (34)

It seems quite strange to me that one doesn't see what an education without the humanities is doing to man. He loses his connection with his family, his connection with his whole past—the whole stem, the tribe—that past in which man has always lived. We think that we are born today *tabula rasa* without a history, but man has always lived in the myth.

To think that man is born without a history within himself—that is a disease. It is absolutely abnormal, because man is not born every day. He is born into a specific historical setting with specific historical qualities, and therefore, he is only complete when he has a relation to these things. If you are growing up with no connection from the past, it is like being born without eyes and ears, and trying to perceive the external world with accuracy. (1)

Civilization does not consist in progress as such and in mindless destruction of the old values, but in developing and refining the good that has been won. (53)

Science is not a perfect instrument, but it is a superb and invaluable tool that works harm only when it is taken as an end itself. Science must serve; it errs when it usurps the throne. It must be ready to serve all its branches, for each, because of its insufficiency, has need of support from the others.

Science is the tool of the Western mind, and with it one can open more doors than with bare hands. It is part and parcel of our understanding, and it obscures our insight only when it claims that the understanding it conveys is the only kind there is. (84)

Eternal truth needs a human language that alters with the spirit of the times. The primordial images undergo ceaseless transformation and yet remain ever the same, but only in a new form can they be understood anew. Always they require a new interpretation if, as each formulation becomes obsolete, they are not to lose their spellbinding power.

What is it about "new wine in old bottles?" Where are the answers to the spiritual needs and troubles of a new epoch? And where the knowledge to deal with the psychological problems raised by the development of modern consciousness? Never before has "eternal" truth been faced with such a hubris of will and power. (63)

In this age of Americanization, it seems to me that we are only at the threshold of a new spiritual epoch. I do not wish to pass myself off as a prophet, but one can hardly attempt to sketch the spiritual problem of modern man without mentioning the longing for rest in a period of unrest, the longing for security in an age of insecurity. It is from need and distress that new forms of existence arise, and not from idealistic requirements or mere wishes.

The crux of the spiritual problem today is to be found in the fascination which the psyche holds for modern man. If we are pessimistic, we shall call it a sign of decadence; if we are optimistically inclined, we shall see it in the promise of a far-reaching spiritual change in the Western world. (90)

Sooner or later, it will be found that nothing really new happens in history. There could be talk of something really novel only if the unimaginable happened: if reason, humanity and love won a lasting victory. (70)

## ADVICE FOR SUCCESSFUL LIVING

Your life is what you try to live. Nobody can live it for you or instead of you. If I should try to put you through something, it would be my life and not yours. When you die, nobody else will die for you or instead of you. It will be entirely and exclusively your own affair. (3)

It is a well-known fact that the "simple life" cannot be faked. . . . Only what is really oneself has the power to heal. (89)

If your work now gives you some joy and satisfaction, you must cultivate it, just as you should cultivate everything that gives you some joy in being alive.

We live in order to attain the greatest possible amount of spiritual development and self-awareness. As long as life is possible, even if only in a minimal degree, you should hang onto it, in order to scoop it up for the purpose of conscious development. (3)

The least of things with a meaning is always worth more in life than the greatest of things without it. (13)

The fundamental error persists in the public that there are definite answers, "solutions," or views which need only be uttered in order to spread the necessary light. But the most beautiful truth—as history has shown a thousand times—is no use at all unless it has become the innermost experience and possession of the individual. (36)

Every unequivocal, so-called clear answer always remains stuck in the head, but only very rarely does it penetrate to the heart. The needful thing is not to *know* the truth, but to *experience* it. Not to have an intellectual conception of things, but to find our way to the inner, and perhaps wordless, irrational experience—that is the great problem. Nothing is more fruitless than talking of how things must or should be, and nothing is more important than finding the way to these far-off goals. (3)

When we allow ourselves to be irritated out of our wits by something, let us not suppose that the cause of our irritation lies simply and solely outside us, in the irritating thing or person. In that way, we simply endow them with the power to put us into the state of irritation, and possibly into one of insomnia or indigestion. We then turn around and unhesitatingly condemn the object of offense, while all the time we are raging against an unconscious part of ourselves which is projected into the exasperating object. (31)

There are, besides the gifts of the head, also those of the heart, which are no whit less important, although they may easily be overlooked because in such cases the head is often the weaker organ. And yet people of this kind sometimes contribute more to the well-being of society, and are more valuable, than those with other talents. (32)

We should not pretend to understand the world only by the intellect; we apprehend it just as much by feeling.

Therefore the judgment of the intellect is, at best, only a half-truth, and must, if it be honest, also admit its inadequacy. (56)

Professor Walter Clark of Harvard University* whom I know personally . . . is a very introverted man who must be approached with the politeness due to animals in the bush: that is, one must act as if one had not seen him and must talk softly and slowly so as not to scare him off. It is also advisable to whistle before going into the forest so that the rhinos won't be startled out of their slumbers, but are gently and melodiously prepared for your coming and have time to make themselves scarce. (3)

If you do not go along with the unconscious properly, that is, if it finds no expression through consciousness and conscious action, it piles up libido in the body and this leads to physical [weaknesses]. (3)

I was very interested in your news of the Maharishi. I'm well aware of the fact that my very Western criticism of such a phenomenon as the Maharishi was rather upsetting to you. I consider a man's life lived for 65 years in perfect balance as most unfortunate. I'm glad that I haven't chosen to live such a miracle. It is so utterly inhuman that I can't see for the life of me any fun in it.

It is surely *wonderful*, but think of being wonderful year in year out! (3)

---

*A professor of Sanskrit, with whom Jung had several stimulating talks during his visit to Harvard in 1936.

You get nowhere with theories. Try to be simple and always take the next step. You needn't see it in advance, but you can look back at it afterwards. There is no "how" of life, one just does it.

So climb down from the mountain of your humility and follow your nose. That is *your* way and the straightest. (3)

If one could arrive at the truth by learning the words of wisdom, then the world would have been saved already in the remote times of Lao-tze. . . . There is little use in teaching wisdom. At all events, wisdom cannot be taught by words. It is only possible by personal contact and by immediate experience.

The great and almost insurmountable difficulty consists in the question of the ways and means to induce people to make the indispensable psychological experiences that open their eyes to the underlying truth. [That] truth is one and the same everywhere. (3)

Your questions are unanswerable because you want to know how one ought to live. One lives as one can. There is no single, definite way which is prescribed for him or would be the proper one. [That] way fits in with the average way of humanity in general.

But if you want to go your individual way, it is the way you make for yourself, which is never prescribed, which you do not know in advance, and which simply comes into being of itself when you put one foot in front of the other. If you always do the next thing that needs to be done, you will go most safely and sure-footedly along the path prescribed by your unconscious. (3)

Everything that is necessary can be lived if only you will stand by yourself and endure things without grumbling. You should always tell yourself: that's how it is, and there's nothing I can do about it. Everything that will, or must be, comes without your doing, and you have only to hold your own in order to come through the darkness of human existence.

Too strong a dependence on the outside, and too dynamic a view of the inside, stem essentially from your desire, intention, and will, which you should push into the background a little for the sake of what really concerns you: holding your own in the chaos of this world. (3)

Sarcasm is the means by which we hide our hurt feelings from ourselves. (3)

If power symptoms creep into the work that is done round you, then diminish your own power and let others have more responsibility. It will teach you a very sound lesson. They will learn that more power and more influence bring more suffering, as you yourself are learning under the present conditions.

One should not assert one's power as long as the situation is not so dangerous that it needs violence. Power that is constantly asserted works against itself, and it is asserted when one is afraid of losing it. One should not be afraid of losing it. One gains more peace through losing power. (3)

I am sorry you are so miserable. "Depression" means literally "being forced downwards." This can happen even when you don't consciously have any feeling at all of being "on top."

If I had to live in a foreign country, I would seek one or

two people who seemed amiable and would make myself useful to them, so that libido came from outside, even though in a somewhat primitive form, say of a dog wagging its tail. I would raise animals and plants and find joy in their thriving. I would surround myself with beauty—no matter how primitive and artless—objects, colors, sounds. I would eat and drink well.

When the darkness grows denser, I would penetrate to its very core and ground, and would not rest until amid the pain a light appeared to me. Nature reverses herself. I would turn in rage against myself and with the heat of my rage I would melt in my lead. I would renounce everything and engage in the lowest activities should my depression drive me to violence. I would wrestle with the dark angel until he dislocated my hip. For he is also the light and the blue sky which he withholds from me.

Anyway, that is what *I* would do. What others would do is another question, which I cannot answer. But for you too there is an instinct either to back out of it, or to go down to the depths. But no half-measures or half-heartedness. (3)

No one can make history who is not willing to risk everything for it, to carry the experiment with his own life through to the bitter end, and to declare that his life is not a continuation of the past, but a new beginning. Mere continuation can be left to the animals, but inauguration is the prerogative of man, the one thing he can boast of that lifts him above the beasts. (86)

The vast majority of people are quite incapable of putting themselves individually into the mind of another. This is indeed a singularly rare art, and, truth to tell, it does not take us very far. Even the man whom we think we know best and who assures us himself that we understand him through and through is at bottom a stranger to us. He is *different*. The most we can do, and the best, is to have at least some inkling of his otherness, to respect it, and to guard against the outrageous stupidity of wishing to interpret it. (89)

Error is just as important a condition of life's progress as truth. (79)

In this overpoweringly humdrum existence, alas, there is little out of the ordinary that is healthy, and not much room for conspicuous heroism. Not that heroic demands are never put to us: on the contrary, and this is just what is so irritating and irksome—the banal everyday makes banal demands on our patience, our devotion, perseverance, self-sacrifice; and for us to fulfill these demands (as we must) humbly and without courting applause through heroic gestures, a heroism is needed that cannot be seen from the outside. It does not glitter, is not belauded, and it always seeks concealment in everyday attire. (81)

[Too often] we limit ourselves to the [easily] attainable, and this means renouncing all our other psychic potentialities. One man loses a valuable piece of his past, another a valuable piece of his future. Everyone can call to mind friends or schoolmates who were promising and idealistic youngsters, but who, when we meet them again years later, seem to have grown dry and cramped in a narrow mold. (74)

Be the man through whom you wish to influence others. Mere talk has always been counted hollow, and there is no trick, however artful, by which this simple truth can be evaded in the long run. The fact of being convinced and not the thing we are convinced of—that is what has always, and at all times, worked. (51)

Disappointment, always a shock to the feelings, is not only the mother of bitterness but the strongest possible incentive to a differentiation of feeling. The failure of a pet plan, the disappointing behavior of someone one loves, can supply the impulse either for a more-or-less brutal outburst of affect or for a modification and adjustment of feeling, and hence, for its higher development.

This culminates in wisdom if feeling is supplemented by reflection and rational insight. Wisdom is never violent: where wisdom reigns, there is no conflict between thinking and feeling. (41)

To strive for perfection is a high ideal. But I say: "Fulfill something you are able to fulfill rather than run after what you will never achieve." Nobody is perfect. Remember the biblical saying, "None is good but God alone" and nobody can be. It is an illusion. We can modestly strive to fulfill ourselves and to be as complete human beings as possible, and that will give us trouble enough. (5)

Doubtless there are exceptional people who are able to sacrifice their entire life to a particular formula; but for most of us, such exclusiveness is impossible in the long run. (56)

Brooding is a sterile activity which runs around in a circle, never reaching a sensible goal. It is not work but a weakness, even a vice. On the other hand, when you've got the blues, it is legitimate to make yourself an object of serious study, just as you can earnestly search your conscience without lapsing into moral weakness.

Anyone who is in bad odor with himself or feels in need of improvement—anyone who, in brief—wishes to "grow," must take counsel with himself. For unless you change yourself inwardly too, outward changes in the situation are either wordless or actually harmful. (25)

We must be able to let things happen in the psyche. For us, this is an art of which most people know nothing. Consciousness is forever interfering, helping, correcting, and negating, never leaving the psychic processes to grow in peace. It would be simple enough, if only simplicity were not the most difficult thing. (84)

All the greatest and most important problems of life are fundamentally insoluble. They must be so, for they express the necessary polarity inherent in every self-regulating system. They can never be solved, but only outgrown. (84)

People will do anything, no matter how absurd, in order to avoid facing their own souls. They will practice Indian yoga and all its exercises, observe a regimen of diet, learn theosophy by heart, or mechanically repeat mystic texts from the literature of the whole world—all because they cannot get on with themselves and have not the slightest faith that anything useful could come out of their own souls. (58)

Psychological treatment cannot rid you of the basic facts of your nature; it can only give you the necessary insight, and only to the extent that you are capable of it. There are countless people with an inferior extraversion, or with too much introversion, or with too little money who . . . must plod along through life under such conditions. These conditions are not diseases but normal difficulties of life. (3)

Caution has its place, no doubt, but we cannot refuse our support to a serious venture which challenges the whole of the personality. If we oppose it, we are trying to suppress what is best in man—his daring and his aspirations. And should we succeed, we should only have stood in the way of that invaluable experience which must have given a meaning to life. What would have happened if Paul had allowed himself to be talked out of his journey to Damascus? (64)

Everything good is costly, and the development of personality is one of the most costly of all things. It is a matter of saying yea to oneself, of taking oneself as the most serious of tasks, of being conscious of everything that one does, and keeping it constantly before one's eyes in all its dubious aspects: truly a task that taxes us to the utmost. (84)

What happens to a person is characteristic of him. He represents a pattern and all the pieces fit. One by one, as his life proceeds, they fall into place according to some predestined plan. (8)

The great decisions in human life usually have far more to do with the instincts and other mysterious unconscious factors than with conscious will and well-meaning reasonableness. The shoe that fits one person pinches another; there is no universal recipe for living. Each of us carries his own life-form within him—an irrational form which no other can outbid. (13)

Suffering that is not understood is hard to bear, while on the other hand, it is often astounding to see how much a person can endure when he understands the why and the wherefore. A philosophical or religious view of the world enables him to do this, and such views prove to be, at the very least, psychic methods of healing if not of salvation. (42)

Life demands for its completion and fulfillment a balance between joy and sorrow. But because suffering is positively disagreeable, people naturally prefer not to ponder how much fear and sorrow fall to the lot of man. So they speak soothingly about progress and the greatest possible happiness, forgetting that happiness itself is poisoned if the measure of suffering has not been fulfilled. (65)

To find happiness in the spirit one must be possessed of a "spirit" to find happiness in. A life of ease and security has convinced everyone of all the material joys, and has even compelled the spirit to devise new and better ways to material welfare, but it has never *produced* spirit. Probably only suffering, disillusion, and self-denial do that. (70)

It is much better to feel that one is not perfect, then one feels much better. (5)

It is often tragic to see how blatantly [one] bungles his own life and the lives of others, yet remains totally incapable of seeing how much the whole tragedy originates in himself, and how he continually feeds it and keeps it going. (14)

Every one of us gladly turns away from his problems, if possible, they must not be mentioned, or better still, their existence is denied. We wish to make our lives simple, certain, and smooth, and for that reason problems are taboo. We want to have certainties and no doubts—results and no experiments—without even seeing that uncertainties can arise only through doubt and results only through experiment. The artful denial of a problem will not produce conviction; on the contrary, a wider and higher consciousness is required to give us the certainty and clarity we need. (74)

Instead of waging war on himself, it is surely better for a man to learn to tolerate himself, and to convert his inner difficulties into real experiences instead of expending them in useless fantasies. Then at least he lives, and does not waste his life in fruitless struggles.

If people can be educated to see the lowly side of their own natures, it may be hoped that they will also learn to understand and to love their fellow men better. A little less hypocrisy and a little more tolerance toward oneself can only have good results in respect for our neighbor. For we are all too prone to transfer to our fellows the injustice and violence we inflict upon our own natures. (91)

Only a fool is interested in other people's guilt, since he cannot alter it. The wise [person] learns only from his own guilt. He will ask himself: Who am I that all this should happen to me? To find the answer to this fateful question, he will look into his own heart. (58)

To the extent that a [person] is untrue to the law of his being and does not rise to [the heights of his] personality, he has failed to realize his life's meaning. (26)

[Profound] experiences cannot be made. They happen—yet fortunately their independence of man's activity is not absolute but relative. We can draw closer to them—that much lies within our human reach. There are ways which bring us nearer to living experience, yet we should beware of calling these ways "methods." The very word has a deadening effect. The way to experience, moreover, is anything but a clever trick: rather a venture which requires us to commit ourselves with our whole being. (64)

It must be admitted that a fit of rage or a sulk has its secret attractions. Were that not so, most people would long since have acquired a little wisdom. (17)

There are experiences which one must go through and for which reason is no substitute. Such experiences are often of inestimable value. (79)

An inexperienced youth thinks that one can let the old people go, because not much more can happen to them anyway; they have their lives behind them and are no better than petrified pillars of the past.

But it is a great mistake to suppose that the meaning of life is exhausted with the period of youth and expansion: that, for example, a woman who has passed the menopause is "finished." The afternoon of life is just as full of meaning as the morning, only its meaning and purpose are different. (81)

Your standpoint seems to coincide with that of our medieval mystics, who tried to dissolve themselves in God. You all seem to be interested in how to get back to the self, instead of looking for what the self wants you to do in the world, where—for the time being at least—we are located, presumably for a certain purpose. . . .

Nobody can be more convinced of the importance of the self than me. But as a young man does not stay in his father's house but goes out into the world, so I don't look back to the self, but collect it out of manifold experiences and put it together again. What I have left behind, seemingly lost, I meet in everything that comes my way. (3)

If you sum up what people tell you about their [growth] experiences, you can formulate it this way: they came to themselves, they could accept themselves, they were able to become reconciled to themselves, and thus were reconciled to adverse circumstances and events. This is almost like what used to be expressed by saying: he has made his peace with God, he has sacrificed his own will, he has submitted himself to the will of God. (60)

That the greatest effort comes from the smallest causes has become patently clear not only in physics but in the field of psychological research as well. How often in the critical moments of life everything hangs on what appears to be a mere nothing! (92)

Life is crazy and meaningful at once. And when we do not laugh over the one aspect and speculate about the other, life is exceedingly drab, and everything is reduced to the littlest scale. Then there is little sense and little non-sense, either. (19)

# LIST OF SOURCES

1. *Dialogue with C. G. Jung.* Edited by Richard Evans. New York: Praeger, 1981.

2. *C. G. Jung Speaking: Interviews and Encounters.* Edited by William McGuire and R. F. C. Hall. Princeton: Princeton University Press, 1977.

3. C. G. Jung: *Letters.* Volume 1: 1906–1950. Volume 2: 1951–1961. Selected and edited by Gerhard Adler. In collaboration with Aniela Jaffé. Translated from the German by R. F. C. Hull. Princeton: Princeton University Press, 1975.

4. C. G. Jung. *Analytical Psychology: Its Theory and Practice (The Tavistock Lectures).* New York: Vintage, 1970.

5. C. G. Jung. *Man and His Symbols. Garden City, New York:* Doubleday, 1964.

6. C. G. Jung. *Memories, Dreams, and Reflections.* Recorded and edited by Aniela Jaffé. Translated by Richard and Clara Winston. New York: Random House, 1963.

7. Face to Face: BBC Interview with John Freeman, 1959. In Hugh Burnett, *Face to Face,* 1964.

8. "Men, Women, and God." *Daily Mail* (London), April 28–29, 1955.

9. "Roosevelt 'Great' in Jung's Analysis." *New York Times,* October 4, 1936.

The following selections from Jung's Collected Works (CW) were also used. The relevant volume after the title of each selection is identified.

10. General Problems of Psychotherapy, CW 16.
11. Principles of Practical Psychotherapy, CW 16.

12. After the Catastrophe, CW 10.

13. The Aims of Psychotherapy, CW 16.

14. Aion, CW 9, Part II.

15. Analytical Psychology and Education, CW 17.

16. Analytical Psychology and Weltanschauung, CW 8.

17. Answer to Job, CW 11.

18. Archaic Man, CW 10.

19. Archetypes of the Collective Unconscious, CW 9.

20. Basel Seminar, 1934, CW 18.

21. Basic Postulates of Analytical Psychology, CW 8.

22. Brother Klaus, CW 11.

23. Foreword by Jung to *Die Anima als Schickalsproblem des Mannes* by Cornelia Brunner, CW 18.

24. Epilogue by Jung to *L'homme à la découverte de son âme* by Roland Cahen, CW 18.

25. Depth Psychology and Self-Knowledge, CW 18.

26. The Development of Personality, CW 17.

27. Psychological commentary by Jung, *The Tibetan Book of the Dead* by W. Y. Evans-Wentz, CW 11.

28. Psychological commentary by Jung, *The Tibetan Book of the Great Liberation* by W. Y. Evans-Wentz, CW 11.

29. Flying Saucers: A Modern Myth of Things Seen in the Skies, CW 10.

30. Freud and Jung: Contrasts, CW 4.

31. General Aspects of Dream Psychology, CW8.

32. The Gifted Child, CW 17.

33. Good and Evil in Analytical Psychology, CW 10.

34. Foreword by Jung, *The Way of All Women* by Esther Harding, CW 18.

35. In Memory of Sigmund Freud, CW 15.

36. Foreword to *Seelenprobleme der Gegenwart,* CW 18.

37. Review by Jung, *La Révolution Mondiale* by Count Hermann Keyserling, CW 10.

38. Introduction by Jung, *Secret Way of the Mind* by W. M. Kranefeldt, CW 4.

39. Marriage as a Psychological Relationship, CW 17.

40. The Meaning of Psychology for Modern Man, CW 10.

41. Mysterium Coniunctionis, CW 14.

42. Statement by Jung for publisher's brochure, *Die Reden Gotamo Buddhos* by Karl Eugen Neumann, CW 18.

43. On the Nature of Dreams, CW 8.

44. On the Nature of the Psyche, CW 8.

45. On Psychic Energy, CW 8.

46. On the Relationship of Analytical Psychology to Poetry, CW 15.

47. Paracelsus, CW 15.

48. Paracelsus as a Spiritual Phenomenon, CW 13.

49. The Philosophical Tree, CW 13.

50. The Practical Use of Dream Analysis, CW 16.

51. Problems of Modern Psychotherapy, CW 16.

52. Psychic Conflicts in a Child, CW 17.

53. A Psychological Approach to the Dogma of the Trinity, CW 11.

54. Psychological Aspects of the Mother Archetype, CW 9, Part I.

55. The Psychological Foundations of Belief in Spirits, CW 8.

56. Psychological Types, CW 6.

57. Psychological Typology, CW 6.

58. Psychology and Alchemy, CW 12.

59. Psychology and Literature, CW 15.

60. Psychology and Religion, CW 11.

61. The Psychology of Eastern Meditation, CW 11.

62. The Psychology of the Child Archetype, CW 9, Part I.

63. The Psychology of the Transference, CW 16.

64. Psychotherapists or the Clergy, CW 11.

65. Psychotherapy and a Philosophy of Life, CW 16.

66. Psychotherapy Today, CW 16.

67. The Real and the Surreal, CW 8.

68. The Realities of Practical Psychotherapy, CW 16.

69. Religion and Psychology: A Reply to Martin Buber, CW 18.

70. Return to the Simple Life, CW 18.

71. Some Crucial Points in Psychoanalysis: A Correspondence Between Dr. Jung and Dr. Löy, CW 4.

72. The Soul and Death, CW 8.

73. Spirit and Life, CW 8.

74. The Stages of Life, CW 8.

75. The State of Psychotherapy Today, CW 10.

76. The Structure of the Psyche, CW 8.

77. Foreword by Jung, *An Introduction to Zen Buddhism* by D. T. Suzuki, CW 11.

78. Symbols of Transformation, CW 5.

79. The Theory of Psychoanalysis, CW 4.

80. Transformational Symbolism in the Mass, CW 11.

81. On the Psychology of the Unconscious, CW 7.

82. The Undiscovered Self, CW 10.

83. What India Can Teach Us, CW 10.

84. Commentary by Jung, *The Secret of the Golden Flower* by Richard Wilhelm, CW 13.

85. Review by Jung, *Die sexuelle Not* by F. Wittels, CW 18.

86. Woman in Europe, CW 10.

87. Wotan, CW 10.

88. Instinct and the Unconscious, CW 8.

89. The Relations between the Ego and the Unconscious, CW 7.

90. The Spiritual Problem of Modern Man, CW 10.

91. New Paths in Psychology, CW 7.

92. The Phenomenology of the Spirit in Fairy Tales, CW 9, Part 1.

93. Foreword by Jung, *Von de inneren Welt des Menschen* by Frances G. Wickes, CW 18.

94. What Is Psychotherapy? CW 16.

95. Individual Dream Symbolism in Relation to Alchemy, CW 12.

96. The Meaning of Psychology for Modern Man, CW 10.

97. Concerning the Archetypes, with Special Reference to the Anima Concept, CW 9, Part 1.

# RESOURCES

## BIOGRAPHIES

Bennet, Edward. *Jung.* London: Barrie & Rockliff, 1961.

Brome, Vincent. *Jung: Man and Myth.* London: Macmillan, 1978.

Franz, Marie-Louise, von. *C. G. Jung: His Myth in Our Time.* Translated by William Kennedy. New York: Putnam, 1975.

Hannah, Barbara. *C. G. Jung: His Life and Work: A Biographical Memoir.* New York: Putnam, 1976.

Jaffé, Aniela. *C. G. Jung: Word and Image.* Princeton: Princeton University Press, 1979.

Jung, Carl G. *Memories, Dreams, and Reflections.* Edited by Aniela Jaffe and translated by Richard and Clara Winston. New York: Vintage, 1989.

McLynn, Frank. *Carl Gustav Jung.* New York: St. Martin's Press, 1996.

Stern, Paul. *C. G. Jung: The Haunted Prophet.* New York: Braziller, 1976.

Storr, Anthony. *Jung.* London: Fantana, 1973.

Van der Post, Lauren. *Jung and the Story of Our Time.* New York: Pantheon, 1975.

## COLLECTED LETTERS

*C. G. Jung Letters.* Selected and edited by Gerhard Adler in Collaboration with Aniela Jaffe. Translated by R. F.C. Hull, 2 volumes. Princeton: Princeton University Press, 1975.

*The Freud–Jung Letters.* Edited by William McGuire. Translated by Ralph Manheim & R. F. C. Hull. Princeton: Princeton University Press, 1974.

### JUNG IN DIALOGUE

*C. G. Jung Speaking: Interviews and Encounters.* Edited by William McGuire & R. F. C. Hull. Princeton: Princeton University Press, 1977.
*Dialogue with C. G. Jung.* Edited by Richard Evans. New York: Praeger, 1981.

### ANTHOLOGIES OF JUNG'S MAJOR WRITINGS

C. G. Jung. *Psychological Reflections.* Edited by Jolande Jacobi & R. F. C. Hull. Princeton: Princeton University Press, 1978.
*The Portable Jung.* Edited by Joseph Campbell. Translated by R. F. C. Hull. New York: Penguin, 1971.

### THE COLLECTED WORKS

*The Collected Works of C. G. Jung,* 21 volumes. Edited by Herbert Read, Michael Fordham & Gerhard Adler. Princeton: Princeton University Press, 1953–1983.

# INDEX

## About the Editor

Edward Hoffman, Ph.D., is a licensed clinical psychologist in New York City. He received his B.A. in psychology from Cornell University and his master's degrees and doctorate from the University of Michigan. Dr. Hoffman is the author/editor of more than a dozen books in psychology and related fields, including major biographies of Abraham Maslow and Alfred Adler. He is a consulting editor of the *Journal of Humanistic Psychology* and has lectured internationally on motivational and organizational issues in this field. His books have been translated into Chinese, French, German, Japanese, Korean, Spanish, and Thai.